D0231493

The fisherman's guide to
Game
Fishing

Marshall Cavendish London & New York

Published by Marshall Cavendish Books Limited
58 Old Compton Street
London W1V 5PA

©Marshall Cavendish Limited 1977, 1978, 1979

This material was first published by
Marshall Cavendish Limited in the
publication *Fisherman's Handbook*

First Printed in 1979

Printed in Great Britain

ISBN 0 85685 643 6

Introduction

During the last twenty years the popularity of game fishing has increased, aided by the stocking of man-made waters with pond-reared fish. This has done much to bring the sport to a far wider group of people than was formerly possible.

The Fisherman's Guide to Game Fishing is concerned with all aspects of the sport under three main headings. The book begins with the species sought by the game fisherman, each one is considered with reference to its habitat, characteristics and life-cycle. This is followed by a section dealing with tackle—both equipment of a primary nature and the ancillaries required such as fly boxes and clothing. Various types of fly and the lines used to fish them are also discussed, as are new fly patterns and tube flies, plus enough information to enable the enthusiast to begin tying his own flies. Finally the heart of the book, the techniques section, deals with methods of fishing. Beginning with the various styles of casting and progressing to more specialised chapters concerned with the various problems posed when fishing different kinds of water, this section includes information on specific problems, such as fly fishing from a boat and trout autopsies.

The Fisherman's Guide to Game Fishing presents areas of interest to suit a wide range of enthusiasts from the beginner to the experienced fly fisherman.

Contents

Game Fishing

Arthur Ogelsley

Salmon

The Atlantic salmon (*Salmo salar*) is one of the most mysterious fish in the world. Considered by many to be king of fish, its reputation as a great and powerful fighter, its great stamina and unusual life-cycle is still fascinating despite our increased knowledge.

Egg fertilization

The salmon egg or 'ova' is generally laid by the parent hen fish in November and December. Scooping out a hollow or 'redd' in the stones she quietly lays her eggs while an attendant male covers them with milt. Fertilization of the covered eggs takes place fairly quickly and it is not long before the female use her broad tail to cover the fragile eggs with loose stones. Unless disturbed, or subjected to excessive floods, the eggs are safe from predators and silting and it will only now be a matter of approximately 90 to 120 days before the new life is born.

The salmon starts its life as a minute egg— the size of a small pea—nestling under loose stones and gravel in the upland waters of the classic salmon rivers or small Highland

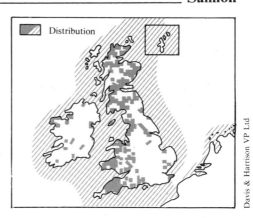

Distribution

Davis & Harrison VP Ltd

Rod Sutterby

Habitat

The salmon, Salmo salar, *is sought by the angler as it makes its way upstream to spawn in the area where it began life. The River Barrow (below), rising in the Slieve Bloom Mountains, is such a water.*

Bait

The range of salmon flies is enormous. Popular patterns are Brown Turkey, Hairy Mary. Worm, lures and shrimps are also used.

Mike Prichard

Salmon

(Left) Salmon parr (the large fish here is perhaps a trout parr) can spend four years feeding in a river before going down to the sea as a smolt. In the sea, the salmon feed well on fish and crustaceans. At between three and five years the smolt is known as a grilse. It is then ready to return to its home redds to breed. (Right) The Spey, shown here at Castle Grant, is one of the great classic salmon rivers of Britain.

Kinns & Ward/Natural Science Photos

burns. Approximately 12 to 15 weeks following fertilization, depending on water temperature, a minute fish or 'alevin' will emerge from the egg. It is then sustained for the next six weeks on a small yolk-sac attached to the underside of its body. Once this has been absorbed, the fish must fend for itself. Now, many mortalities can occur.

Once the yolk-sac is absorbed the initial problem for the infant salmon or 'fry' is that of finding food. Early spring can be cold and cheerless. Natural food in many upland, acid streams will be at a premium and the salmon faces the first battle for survival. Sadly, the ravages of nature will kill off a large number of the hatching stock; but those which do find food and resist the attacks of numerous predators still have many pitfalls ahead to overcome. Slowly, however, cheerless spring gives way to softer summer. Hatching flies dance on the water and the salmon 'parr' feed on every available morsel of food to come their way. Another freshwater winter still lies ahead when food will again be at a premium and the small parr must be ever-watchful for herons and a host of other hungry predators.

Given survival and a bit more luck, at the end of a two-year sojourn in the upland streams the young parr slowly acquires a silvery coat. It is now fast approaching the 'smolt' stage. With the first warming of the upland waters—frequently in May—the smolt will instinctively drop downstream to the estuaries and the wide open sea. This too is fraught with danger from predators and unknown pollutants in the lower reaches of many of our rivers. Further losses will occur, and only a few will attain the sanctuary of the deep sea and be lost in its vastness.

Sea-going migrations

This at least was the way it was thought to be until a few years ago. Today, we know some of the sea-going migration routes which British salmon take. It is known, for instance, that many go to the rich feeding grounds off the coast of Greenland. Also, once at sea, a smolt is known to increase its weight by 15 times in less than a year. Thus a small, insignificant fish of five or six ounces can quickly become one of five or six pounds. At this stage of its development it is known as a 'grilse' and it is now capable of reproduction and of making its way back to the river of its birth. Depending on circumstances, however, many of the fish will continue to rove the seas for another year. This may enable them to double or treble their weight and thus reach maturity. A great deal depends on water temperatures and availability of food; but a two-year sea life salmon should reach eight to 10lb. Some salmon, staying up to five years at sea, reach weights of at least 30 or 40lb and more.

Arthur Oglesby

Many of our migrating salmon go north. Some are reputed to go under the Arctic ice—which, mercifully, protects them from the destructive tactics of the commercial fishermen to which they often fall prey.

The urge to reproduce

At some stage in their sea journeys the salmon will develop the overpowering urge to come back to the rivers of their birth, find a mate and reproduce the species. Salmon behaviour in this respect is not uniform and a great deal will depend on the individual river from which the salmon have originally come. On such rivers as the Tweed, Tay, Spey, Dee, Wye and Eden—a lot of fish return in the early spring. Some rivers will, however, have fresh fish in January, but it is little more than speculation why fish enter one river then and others in summer or autumn. Not all salmon are destined to spawn in November or December. What induces a spring-running instinct in one salmon and an autumn return in another still remains a mystery. Much

inconclusive speculation has been generated on the why's and wherefore's of salmon behaviour, but the fish remains enigmatic, with a strong disposition of pleasing itself!

The salmon's trials begin

History provides a lot of clues of when salmon are likely to enter a specific river system. On most rivers of the British Isles the first trial the fish must undergo is to run the gauntlet of the various netting and trapping systems operated in or near the estuary. Sustained high water in the rivers during the early months will ensure good passage for the fish with minimal loss to the commercial operators. At times of low water the fish tend to rove the estuaries waiting for adequate flows and may thus be more likely to suffer capture by the nets on every ebb and flood of the tides. Of course it makes sense for man to crop this valuable resource; but it also demands responsible behaviour from those who take the crop. Unfortunately, the high price of salmon encourages the illegal element to flourish and salmon will continue to be in jeopardy as a species until greater protective measures are introduced.

Shortly before entering the river, the salmon ceases to take food, though the reason for this is unclear. Some authorities say that salmon simply lose all desire for food and that, as a result, the stomach occludes and the fish become incapable of digestion. Others claim that nature causes the gut to atrophy to that food cannot be taken anyway. Whatever the real reason, there is little doubt that salmon in freshwater do not feed in the full sense of the word. Living in freshwater the salmon suffers a slow deterioration. But even if the salmon

did show a desire to feed in freshwater, few of our classical salmon rivers contain sufficient food to sustain them anyway. Certainly on capture in freshwater, nothing is ever found in the salmon's stomach.

The salmon's power and beauty

On entering the river the salmon is beautifully arrayed with a bright silvery mantle—an object of power and beauty, in its prime for both sporting and culinary purposes. Apart from an unidentified and spasmodic disease known as Ulcerative Dermal Necrosis (UDN), the next predator in the chain is the angler. But, as the fish do not feed in freshwater, angling is a very inefficient method fo catching them. There is

(Inset, below) Driven by a powerful and instinctive urge, the salmon comes in from the sea to run upstream, heading for its birthplace. Hazards, such as commercial fishermen, rapids, pollution—and anglers—await the fish.

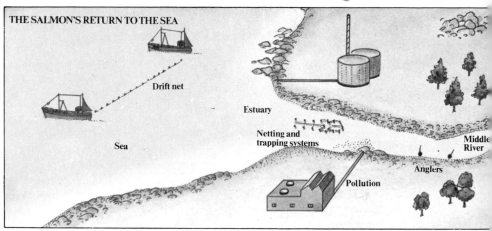

THE SALMON'S RETURN TO THE SEA

Drift net

Estuary

Sea

Netting and trapping systems

Pollution

Anglers

Middle River

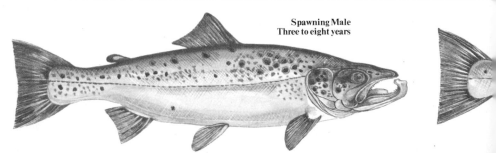

Spawning Male
Three to eight years

(Left) Burrishoole Fishery, Co Mayo, typical of the waters that salmon ascend in order to spawn.
(Below) Life cycle of the salmon. The alevin feeds on the attached yolk-sac until all the nutriment has gone. The tiny fish must then find its own food. After two years in the parr stage the fish, now a smolt, heads for the sea, where it will feed on the rich diet of the salt-water fauna. Once back in freshwater it will not feed.

Irish Tourist Board

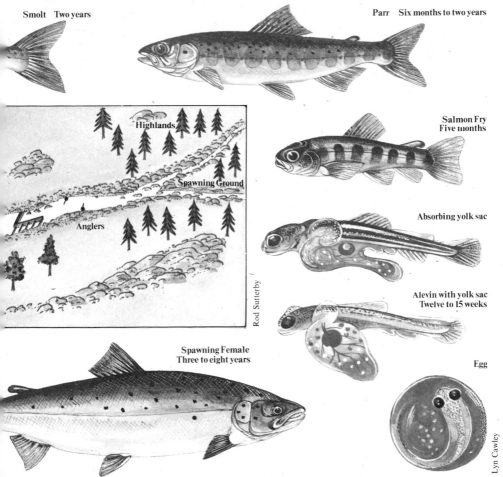

Smolt Two years

Parr   Six months to two years

Highlands

Spawning Ground

Anglers

Rod Sutterby

Salmon Fry
Five months

Absorbing yolk sac

Alevin with yolk sac
Twelve to 15 weeks

Spawning Female
Three to eight years

Egg

Lyn Cawley

G. L. Carlisle

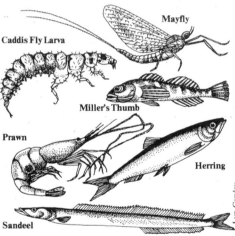

Caddis Fly Larva

Mayfly

Miller's Thumb

Prawn

Herring

Sandeel

Lyn Cawley

Irish Tourist Board

(Top) A salmon ladder on the River Tummell, near Pitlochry, Perthshire. (Above) A popular salmon fly, Jock Scott. (Left) The salmon's natural diet. (Right) The ghillie, just as pleased as the angler, unhooks a fine Irish salmon.

no known bait that will induce them to *feed*, but there are several lures which will, on occasion, induce salmon to take them into their mouths for sufficient time to become hooked. Many fisheries demand a high standard of sportsmanship from their anglers and rents to fish the better beats or stretches are now quite high. In the final resort, however, is is the angler who takes the minimum crop of salmon. Yet it is the same angler who shows greatest concern for the survival of the species. In terms of licence dues, rents and rates, the angler pays a high price for his sport, the highest in all fishing. He also makes the largest financial contribution to the good husbandry of salmon.

On their first entry into freshwater the salmon may be lethargic or active depending on water temperature alone. Cold water induces sluggish response from the fish. Most will be content to move slowly and to stay in the lower reaches of the classic rivers.

Fresh-run salmon

Angling tactics involve making the lure or bait move slowly and at a good depth; but there is always the chance of sport with fresh-run fish. Within 48 hours of their entry into freshwater, the parasitic sea lice will begin to drop from their host. There is no specific time for sea lice to stay alive in freshwater, for they have been known to survive under laboratory conditions for up to seven days.

Most anglers accept the 48-hour theory, so it is a sure sign that when a fish is caught with sea lice on it, it is as fresh a fish as possible.

Experience the best guide

As water temperatures rise, and always provided there are adequate river flows, the fish will be induced to run quickly through the lower beats and into the middle and upper reaches. Here they may be induced to take small flies or lures fished near the surface and they can be much more active. Sometimes it is possible to catch them 50 miles upstream of the estuary with sea lice still on them, but there can be no hard-and-fast rule. Only long experience of a specific river over the seasons will give a glimmer of a clue as to where the fish might be and when.

Despite these movement patterns, there comes a time when all the salmon requires is to be left in peace and quiet. Most will settle up in pools and known lies for long periods throughout the summer. Joined by later-run fish or small summer grilse, most will ignore the flies and lures offered by anglers. While the stock of fish in the pools gradually

increases, the salmon will slowly be burning up energy and losing body weight and girth. By November the salmon having survived the wiles of man and nature will be a sorry-looking creature. The flesh will have wasted away to provide the essential milt and ova which it will shed on the redds. Males will compete with other males for the best spawning placed and the most attractive partner. Some redds will be overcut and nature will also exact a high toll. Following the spawning act, many of the females will drop back into quiet water and recover.

The possessive male

Many male salmon, however, will stay near the redds and fight off other intruders. Many will succumb and die; but, unlike the Pacific salmon, which dies following spawning, there will be many survivors slowly dropping back downstream as spawned salmon or 'kelts' to return to the sea once again. Here, many of these weak and emaciated kelts will fall to marine predators such as seals, and only a few will survive to make the journey again and repeat the act of spawning.

Irish Tourist Board

Brown trout

It could be argued that the brown trout requires little introduction in these days of supermarkets and freezer stores where it is displayed for sale. Most people will have met a hatchery-bred fish on the end of a fork.

Intensive hatchery fish farming, however, should not be condemned. Anglers want to fish waters where there is a good head of quality fish and the restaurateur needs plate-sized trout for the table—the hatcheries supply them both.

Breeding and culling

By selective breeding, and culling out the younger fish for the 'table market', the breeder produces fast growing, healthy fish for planting out as fingerlings or 6in yearlings. Fortunately the stocking authorities also like to plant a good supply of 10-12 in stock fish as well as a sprinkling of two- or three-pounders. All this keeps the fishery healthy and the angler happy. A single season in the wild turns these hatchery-bred fish into tough, hardy, flavoursome and sporting fish.

The brown trout, *Salmo trutta*, is indigenous to Europe, North West Asia, and North Africa. It shows a remarkable diversity of shape and coloration, often according to locality. It can be categorized into two distinct forms which differ chiefly in life style but also in size and colour. The sea-trout is the migratory form. Like the salmon it spends part of its life in the sea feeding well, and putting on weight. It then returns to the river of its birth as it becomes ready to spawn. Once it has done so it drops back to the sea until next year.

The brown trout is the non-migratory form which lives in rivers and lakes. The steeper gradients of the rivers where brown trout survive best are often a long way from the sea, and in many rivers they are separated from the sea by the slower sluggish zones which trout tend to avoid. Often mild pollution also bars the way to the sea. In any event the brown trout has been separated from the sea for many generations and has adopted an entirely freshwater mode of life.

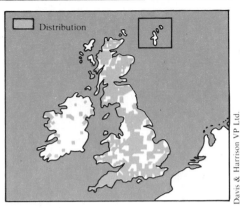

Distribution

Davis & Harrison VP Ltd.

Rod Sutterby

Habitat
The brown trout, Salmo trutta, *is found in fast, clear waters and streams, but it can flourish in lakes and reservoirs.*

Bait
This fish can be caught by all natural baits, but on many waters a fly-fishing-only rule is imposed.

(Below) A quiet, limpid backwater of the River Test renowned for its quality trout fishing.

British Tourist Authority

Bill Howes

The migratory and non-migratory trout are the extreme forms in terms of habit and appearance but there are several distinctive variations which appear in particular locations. These were indeed once considered to be separate and distinct species, or at least sub-species, and were even given scientific names to distinguish their specific status. More recently these fish have been shown to be capable of interbreeding to produce fertile progeny, and they are now regarded as variable members of the same species, now known throughout its indigenous range as *Salmo trutta*.

Local variations

Nevertheless local pride runs high, and the local names persist. Anglers anxious to sample the sporting qualities of these variations will not be disappointed by the Gilaroo trout of the Irish loughs, nor the Loch Leven or Orkney trout of their respective localities.

Where the water has not been ruined by pollution, abstraction, sewerage or canalization, brown trout are to be found in most river systems. They live in the swifter steep gradients where rocky, gravelly or stony bottoms and the swift flow produce the high oxygen requirements of the trout, and provide the kind of spawning facilities upon which their future stocks depend. The

(Above) Fishing for trout in early summer from a quiet bank of Rutland Water in Northamptonshire.
(Below) The natural food of brown trout includes a wide variety of insects, molluscs and crustaceans.

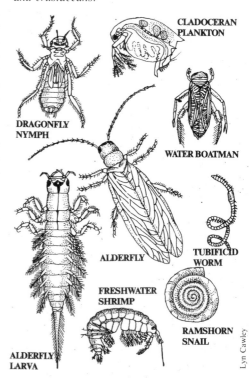

CLADOCERAN PLANKTON

DRAGONFLY NYMPH

WATER BOATMAN

ALDERFLY

TUBIFICID WORM

FRESHWATER SHRIMP

RAMSHORN SNAIL

ALDERFLY LARVA

Lyn Cawley

JUNGLE ALEXANDRA

PETER ROSS

WET FLIES

BLOODY BUTCHER

Lyn Cawley

(Above) Popular wet flies for catching trout include the Bloody Butcher, that was first tied some 150 years ago, the Peter Ross and the Jungle Alexandra.
(Below) Cross-section through a reservoir showing the trout's habitat and food.

slower, sluggish, muddy-bottomed reaches inhabited by coarse fishes are not favoured by trout although the coarse fish angler seeking roach or bream will occasionally take a trout on his worm.

Trout are very much at home in the typical moorland stream or the rocky beck as well as in the traditional chalk streams of Southern England. They also do well in lakes and ponds where the conditions are suitable. The intensive reservoir building programme that has taken place during the post-war years, however, has led to a total redistribution of the species throughout Britain. Many fine new waters have appeared in regions such as the South East and Midlands where few suitable rivers remained for trout. Most of these new waters have been extensively stocked with trout, and good trout fishing is now probably more plentiful and cheaper than it has ever been.

Waters rich in calcium produce prolific weed growth, and this in turn stimulates the growth of numerous insect, mollusc and

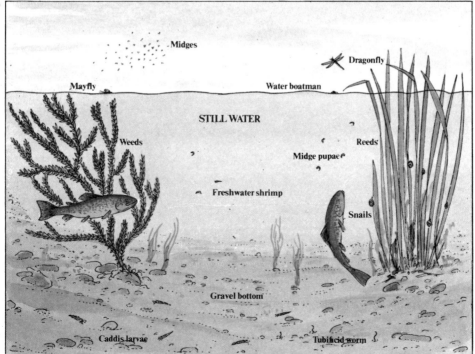

Midges

Dragonfly

Mayfly

Water boatman

STILL WATER

Weeds

Reeds

Midge pupae

Freshwater shrimp

Snails

Gravel bottom

Caddis larvae

Tubificid worm

Rod Sutterby

crustacean stocks. In such waters the generous food supplies favour big, fast-growing fish. Blagdon and Chew reservoirs are good examples and the angler confidently expects to take fish between 2lb and 3lb. With luck he hopes to get the odd four or five-pounder. If he is especially favoured, and suitably skilled, he may net a fish over 6lb or 7lb. The chalk streams of the South also produce excellent fish. The Avon, Kennet, Test and Lambourne rivers are typical examples. In Ireland, Lough Inchiquin and Lough Rea are well known for their high quality of fish. At the other extreme the tiny becks and streams of some northern and western districts produce small, mature, but game and crafty trout up to 8in long.

The rainbow trout

Owing to wise stocking policies most reservoirs in southern England will provide anglers with average fish of about a pound. The occasional two pounder will be taken, and once or twice in a season a three-

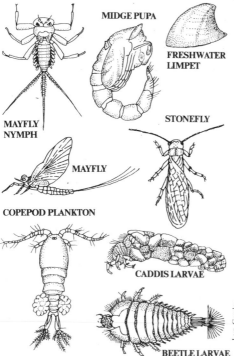

MIDGE PUPA

FRESHWATER LIMPET

MAYFLY NYMPH

STONEFLY

MAYFLY

COPEPOD PLANKTON

CADDIS LARVAE

BEETLE LARVAE

Lyn Cawley

(Above) A typical stretch of fast-flowing trout river at Teesdale.
(Left) A selection of the brown trout's natural food found in fast-flowing waters.
(Below) A cross-section of a highland stream showing the natural habitat and food of the brown trout.

Moss

Caddis larvae

(Below) Artificial flies come in hundreds of different dressings, but generally dry flies are not so highly coloured as wet flies. Olive Dunn, Sedge and the Dark Sedge are examples.

.OLIVE DUNN

SEDGE

DARK SEDGE

DRY FLIES

England Scene

Lyn Cawley

pounder will be recorded in the book. This is good trout fishing by any standards. A bonus for the trout fisherman has been the introduction, alongside the native brown trout, of the American rainbow trout, *Salmo gairdneri,* into most stillwaters. So you may catch either species, and the chief distinguishing feature is that the brown has no spots on its tail.

Brown trout spawn at somewhere between two and four years of age. The eggs vary not only a great deal in size, but also in their incubation period. Research indicates that the time varies according to water temperature. It ranges from 21 weeks at 2°C (36°F) to four weeks at 12°C (54°F). Losses are staggering during this incubation period, and during the first year of life. Estimates vary, but the general view is that of 10,000 eggs produced only about 250 fish survive to the end of the first year. Growth rates vary too. A year-old fish may be between 1in and 5in long, a two-year-old between 4in and 9in, and a three-year-old between 6in and 13in. Hatchery fish have been recorded surviving to 12 years old, but the general run of fish is estimated to live to four or five years before it dies naturally, or is caught by the angler.

Fortunately for the angler the feeding habits of trout do not differ as widely as their growth rates, incubation periods, and maturation ages. Most trout, wherever they

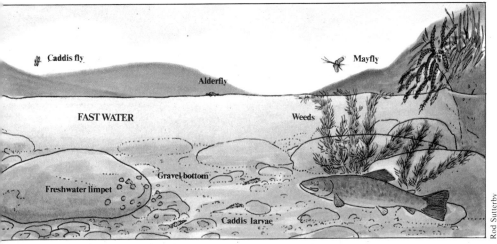

Caddis fly

Alderfly

Mayfly

FAST WATER

Weeds

Gravel bottom

Freshwater limpet

Caddis larvae

Rod Sutterby

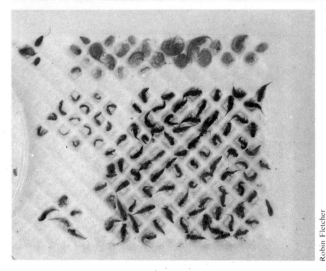

(Left) In order to match the tied fly with the natural on which the trout has been feeding waterside autopsies can be carried out. This can be done either by gutting the fish and emptying the fish's stomach contents into a dish, or by the use of a marrow-spoon inserted down the trout's throat. Here the stomach's contents clearly show that this fish has been feeding on freshwater shrimp, top, and various beetles and insect larvae.

Robin Fletcher

live, obtain most of their food from or near the bottom. They certainly supplement this staple diet with water-borne flies and insects living in or on the surface, or alighting temporarily upon it. They are not fussy about what they eat when hungry and will snap up almost anything which moves, providing they can manage to swallow it. They can be extremely fussy when food supplies are plentiful, and then the angler is hard put to please them.

Trout's haven and base

In rivers the fish tend to select a 'lie' which becomes their territorial base. It usually offers a haven from predators, and is protected from the full force of the current. They have their own territory around this base, and forage freely within it. The stream brings along food supplies regularly, and they probably feed rather more on the surface than their reservoir counterparts. Such a fish will defend its territory from intruders, and each fish in a particular reach knows its own place in the hierarchy or pecking order. If the big fellow succumbs to the angler his place will not be empty for long. The next in succession will occupy it and others will move up in the queue.

Anglers generally know such spots in their own river, and have the advantage that they can often stalk a known fish in a known

place. The disadvantage is often the very clear nature of the stream which discloses any careless move to the fish, and unfortunately 'puts him down'.

The reservoir angler often has the advantage of somewhat coloured water, and a profusion of bankside weed and vegetation. His fish rise less often, but nevertheless patrol their territories, usually giving away their rising spots. Their territories are larger, and may be vacated from time to time as the fish cruise up the wind lanes, or around the margins, in their search for food.

Although trout can be taken on many baits, including the lowly maggot, worm, spinners and lures, the artificial fly is the offering most used to attract this game fish.

Wet and dry flies

Trout are taken on dry and wet flies. The basic difference between these is that the hackles on the dry fly stand out, making it float on the surface, while the wet fly's 'wings' sweep backwards and it is fished below the surface. Wet flies and dry flies come in hundreds of different dressings and the number is added to every season. Some flies represent nothing more than the fly tier's whim and fancy—but they catch trout. Other flies represent small fish, insects and their larvae, spiders and freshwater shrimps (*Gammarus pulex*).

COLOUR VARIATION

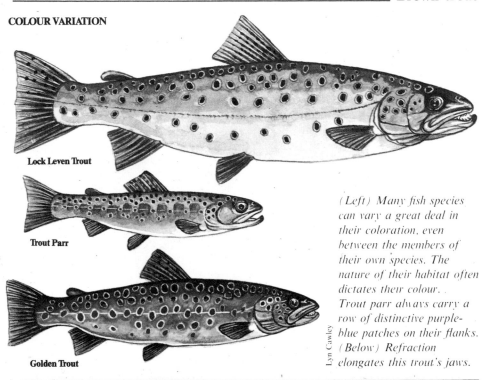

Lock Leven Trout

Trout Parr

Golden Trout

Lyn Cawley

(Left) Many fish species can vary a great deal in their coloration, even between the members of their own species. The nature of their habitat often dictates their colour. Trout parr always carry a row of distinctive purple-blue patches on their flanks. (Below) Refraction elongates this trout's jaws.

F. Dalgety/Camera Press

Rainbow trout

The rainbow trout, *Salmo gairdneri* is a native of the Pacific coast, rivers and lakes of the North American Continent, ranging from the Bering Sea in the north, to the southern Californian coasts in the south. Since 1884 the species has been introduced to suitable waters all over the world with varying degrees of success. In Britain it has rarely bred successfully and in most cases now exists only as a result of continual re-stocking from fish farms which have successfully bred the species by modern stripping techniques.

Rainbow's American habitat

In its American habitat the rainbow fills a niche comparable to that occupied in Britain by our native brown trout. Similarly it exhibits numerous variants (each once believed to be a distinct species) and provides a similar range of migratory and non-migratory fish. Its growth rates vary widely according to type and environment, and it provides excellent sport for anglers. Brown and rainbow trout, are however, of quite

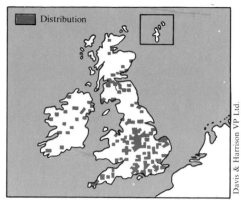

Distribution

Rod Sutterby

Davis & Harrison VP Ltd.

Habitat
The rainbow trout, Salmo gairdneri, *is a North American species introduced into the waters of Britain in the 19th century. The fish has become established in a few waters where the conditions are right for natural breeding.*

Baits
Artificial flies according to time, place, season and water conditions.

Eric Birch

BROWN TROUT
Salmo trutta

RAINBOW TROUT
Salmo gairdneri

BROOK CHAR
Salvelinus fontinalis

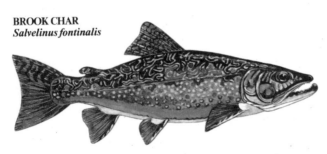

VOMER BONES

BROWN TROUT

RAINBOW TROUT

BROOK CHAR

Lyn Cawley

(Above) Teeth in the upper jaw (called vomerine teeth) are an aid to identifying brown trout, rainbow trout and brook char.
(Left) Related species.

different species—although related to the *Salmo* genus.

Generally a far hardier fish than the brown trout, the rainbow can withstand high temperatures, low oxygen levels, and murky waters. It is also a far more active fish, being a free riser to the fly and living and moving in loose shoals, with a strong urge to migrate upstream for spawning, falling back into lakes or lower reaches for the rest of the season. At the extreme it is anadromous, like sea trout, migrating from dense to less dense water to breed, and enters freshwaters only to spawn.

In appearance it is similar to the brown trout apart from a distinctive wide lateral band of iridescent magenta along the middle flanks. It is usually black spotted, and the spots, unlike those of the brown trout, grow more quickly. Rainbow trout grow to a larger maximum size than the brown trout. It also spawns later than brown trout, and is therefore in excellent condition in British waters at the very end of the season.

Early work on the rainbow
The history, literature and taxonomy of rainbow trout in North America is every bit as confusing as that of its British cousin, the brown trout. Nineteenth century American and European zoologists identified and named a variety of species of trout. In Europe, for example, Gunther described

Bill Howes

(Above) What is the function of the adipose fin? This fleshy appendage seems to serve no purpose, and when removed as a check during population studies it does not affect the fish or grow again.
(Left) The head of a rainbow with the hook still lodged in the angle of the jaws.

G. L. Carlisle

some ten different species each with its own scientific name, while in America a similar number of trout were similarly described by authorities, and named.

During the early part of the present century the zoological view that a species should be regarded primarily as a breeding unit, despite minor physical differences, gained ascendancy. It was shown under laboratory conditions that all the known British trouts were able to produce fertile progeny when cross-bred. More than anything, this led to their re-allocation to a single species *Salmo trutta*. The same sort of study of species in America resulted in an all-American trout being classified into the

species *Salmo gairdneri*. All trout were subsumed under this heading with the single notable exception of the brook trout, which in fact turned out to be a char and now enjoys the separate specific title of *Salvelinus fontinalis*. The char is, however, still commonly known in America as a trout but can be distinguished from the rainbow by its green-brown colour with lighter 'worm-track' patterns on the back, and reddish tinge on the underside. Examination of the vomerine bone on the upper palate will also provide distinguishing features. Rainbow trout have single rows of teeth set in a 'T' shape. Chars, on the other hand, bear only a group or cluster of teeth on this bone. The North American brook trout has also been introduced to some waters in Britain and these should not be confused with either brown or rainbow trout.

Feeding habits

Rainbows normally feed on a very similar diet to brownies. When young they exist on daphnia, cyclops and other infusoria, but

Rainbow trout

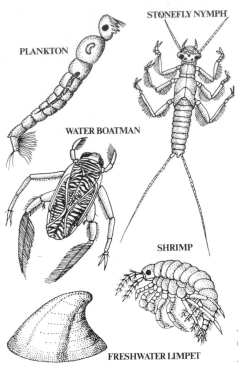

PLANKTON

STONEFLY NYMPH

WATER BOATMAN

SHRIMP

FRESHWATER LIMPET

once past the alevin stage quickly graduate to shrimp and insects, and on to snail and fish fry in addition within a year. Not only are rainbows more prone to rise than brown trout, but they are far more active in their search for food, ranging between the bottom and the surface continuously and taking good advantage of midges, nymphs, mayflies and their larvae, and in the evening on sedges and daddy long legs. In waters where coarse fish fry are plentiful, rainbows soon get used to supplementing their diet with such delicacies. It is not unusual for anglers to find fish of 14in with roach of three or four inches in their stomachs. Such fish become as predatory as pike, and as rainbows move in loose shoals they are sometimes seen driving

(Left) The natural food of the rainbow trout. The fish will also take flies and insects that fall onto the water.
(Below) The rainbow's natural habitat.
(Right) A quiet section of Blagdon, with Bill Howes trying for an April fish.

Lyn Cawley

WATER BEETLES

WEEDS

FRESHWATER SHRIMP

Rod Sutterby

Len Cacutt

shoals of small fish into the shallows where they hunt them down voraciously.

At the other end of the scale, rainbows often rise freely in boisterous weather, feeding well on the surface during high winds, following the wind lanes in large groups and fearlessly rising under the bows of the angler's boat. They will often cruise upwind in such conditions, dropping into the depths when they come to the far shores, and then feed earnestly in mid-water, or on the bottom.

When to use the dry fly

In calmer weather, when the surface is like a millpond and the angler despairs of getting his wet flies to work without creating a heavy wake, the rainbows will often rise maddeningly at midges and other small flies on the surface, ignoring the wet flies offered by the fisherman. Then the dry fly is often useful. Takes are sudden, and the rainbow is usually moving fast when it hits the fly. Smash-takes occur in these conditions, even when the cast is realistically heavy. It behoves the angler to

ensure that his rod is not left pointing at the fly so that such a take is absorbed by the rod when the fish often hooks itself.

The traditional wet fly method

Under normal conditions, with a light popple on the water, and a gentle breeze, the angler is able to fish without the wind interfering with his casting. The broken surface of the water will prevent fish spotting the angler's movements too easily, as well as covering up his mistakes when working the fly. In such conditions the traditional wet fly method is a joy, both from the bank or from a boat. A team of three wet flies is used with a long cast which, fished slowly, presents them at different levels, often enabling the angler to locate the best depth. Sometimes it also indicates the 'taking' fly. Medium casting from the bank, or short lining from a boat can be very productive.

When the fish are dour and not showing, the angler must fish the water, covering as much territory as he can to get fish moving, or locate moving fish. A lure is sometimes

Eric Birch

successful and several patterns should be tried at various depths and different speeds. Sometimes the angler is reduced to 'scratching the bottom' with a leaded lure fished slow. Alternatively, a flasher fished fast may be used. Rainbows can often be tempted when high water temperatures have caused the brown trout to go completely off feeding. They will also move quite fast from comparatively deep water to a tempting fly realistically fished on or near the surface, following it until it is about to break surface.

The buzzer rise

When the buzzer rise occurs in the evening, fish will sip delicately at the nymph or smash at it, leaping out of the water and landing on the nymph with a boil. In late summer, when the sedges are on the water, rainbows will take boldly and hearteningly.

When fish are hooked high in the water they will often leap and splash on the surface from the moment they are hooked. Sometimes it is essential to get the rod point

(Above) Rainbow trout in the 'wild'—which are not stock fish put into waters from fish breeding ponds—do not achieve the high growth rate of the fish produced at Avington. This rainbow, caught from the Wye, one of Britain's leading game rivers, is typical of the fish which breed naturally.

down into the water to sink the line so as to absorb their acrobatics.

Most reservoir anglers welcome the rainbow and the exciting sport it offers in a hundred subtly different ways in different conditions. It can be as coy as the brown trout, and loves to cruise on the surface on hot days, sipping in the green pea-soup which the water often becomes in these conditions. Then it can be maddeningly difficult to tempt.

The increasing use of fish farming is essential if stocks are to be maintained in the face of increasing pressures from anglers, to say nothing of pollution, water abstraction, and commercial netting. These occur on

(Left) A 15lb stock fish which fell to the sunken wet fly. Selective breeding can achieve weights not possible in the wild colonies.
(Below) A typical three-fly team for use on reservoirs. A worm fly lure and Price's Orange Streamer are also shown.

Alan Pearson

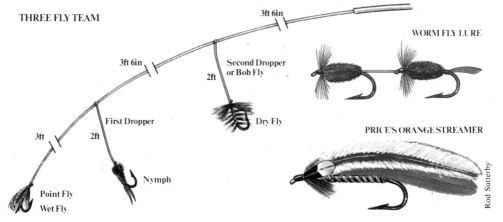

THREE FLY TEAM

3ft 6in

3ft 6in

Second Dropper
or Bob Fly

2ft

First Dropper

Dry Fly

3ft 2ft

Nymph

Point Fly

Wet Fly

DADDY LONG LEGS

WORM FLY LURE

PRICE'S ORANGE STREAMER

Rod Sutterby

both sides of the Atlantic, and as stocks are regenerated from selectively bred fish-farm introduction, it is possible that the local variants will gradually disappear.

In Britain the continual existence of the rainbow is heavily dependent upon the fish farmer. In the vast majority of British waters rainbows become spawn-bound and fail to breed naturally. They can only be maintained by stocking.

Breeding colonies

The exceptions are the Derbyshire Wye, the Chess and the Misbourne, where rainbows have established breeding colonies. They also breed in Blagdon Reservoir in Somerset co-existing with the brown trout.

Rainbows are very suitable for introduction to reservoirs because they live only for four or five seasons, and can be stocked in a range of sizes. In most farm conditions a one-year-old fish may be between 4 and 8in attaining between 6 and 12in in its second year. A third year fish may be between 9 and 16in, and a fourth year fish between 14 and 20in. These are average figures and can be exceeded with suitable feeding and water conditions. A few years ago a 10lb rainbow was exceptional. Recent introductions at Avington fisheries, where fish of 20lb are being produced on high-protein diets, indicate that selective breeding has vastly improved future catches.

Sea trout

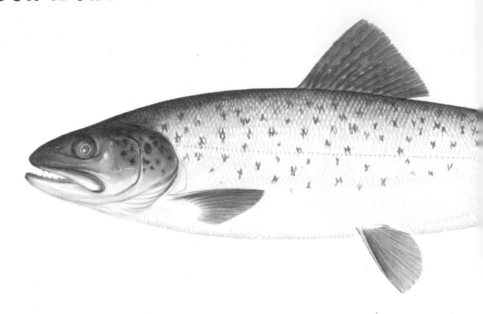

Until recent times it was thought that the sea trout, *Salmo trutta* as it was originally classified, was an independent species, while brown trout were known as *Salmo fario*. Scientific opinion now is that they are both of the species *Salmo trutta*. Even as long ago as 1887 it was asserted that there existed only this latter species of trout in Britain. This uncomplicated classification may satisfy those with a scientific turn of mind, but it does nothing for the angler who finds vast behavioural and environmental differences between the sea trout and the non-migratory 'brownie'.

What, then, is a sea trout? Sadly, a satisfactory answer is not forthcoming and we must accept that the sea trout, for want of factual information, is nothing more than a migratory brown trout. Just what induced the initial migration is little more than pure speculation; but there is on record the scientific opinion that all the family *Salmo* were of marine origin and that it was the last Ice Age which caused some to be landlocked

and others to develop the migratory instinct, perhaps as long ago as 100,000 years.

As with the salmon, therefore, the sea trout's origins are not fully understood. It follows a very similar life pattern to that of the salmon, and there was a time when our sea trout were simply called salmon-trout. Obviously, all the *Salmo* species had similar beginnings and for this reason many angling novices have difficulty distinguishing one from the other. There are differences, however, some subtle, others appreciable.

Sea trout's spawning time

Sea trout usually begin their spawning in October. On average, they are two or three weeks earlier than salmon, but there is no hard and fast rule. November is probably the month of greatest activity but some fish, according to one authority, may spawn throughout the winter. He adds that, although ripe (ready to spawn) sea trout, which have not begun to shed ova or milt, may be seen in January, and very occasionally in February, their spawning

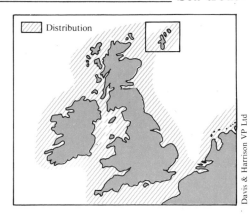

Distribution

Davis & Harrison VP Ltd

Rod Sutterby

Habitat

The sea trout ascend rivers to spawn. Below, silhouetted against an orange sunset, are Leslie Moncrieff and John Goddard, fishing somewhere along the 109-mile Ring of Kerry, a scenic route in South-West Ireland, where prime sea trout fishing may be enjoyed.

Baits

There are numerous sea trout flies, but the species may also be taken on lure and worm.

Mike Prichard

Sea trout

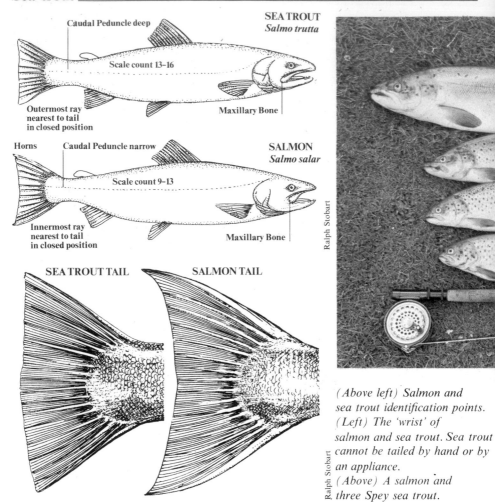

SEA TROUT
Salmo trutta

Caudal Peduncle deep

Scale count 13-16

Outermost ray
nearest to tail
in closed position

Maxillary Bone

Horns Caudal Peduncle narrow

SALMON
Salmo salar

Scale count 9-13

Innermost ray
nearest to tail
in closed position

Maxillary Bone

SEA TROUT TAIL   SALMON TAIL

Ralph Stobart

Ralph Stobart

*(Above left) Salmon and
sea trout identification points.
(Left) The 'wrist' of
salmon and sea trout. Sea trout
cannot be tailed by hand or by
an appliance.
(Above) A salmon and
three Spey sea trout.*

season is generally shorter than that of the salmon, and much shorter than that of non-migratory trout.

Sea trout prefer smaller gravel than salmon for the construction of the redd in which the eggs are laid and fertilized, and, like salmon, find sand and mud unsuitable. Some will spawn in water barely deep enough to cover their backs, and they may be found in many small Scottish Highland burns with access to the larger river systems.

As with the salmon, it is the female sea trout which, with broad sweeps of its tail, makes the redd. Females are said to be able to produce 700–800 eggs for each pound of weight, but this is only a very rough guide. Like salmon, and depending on water temperature, a period of 90–120 days elapses before the eggs hatch. Much the same behavioural and growth pattern as in young salmon then occurs (see earlier chapter) but once the young sea trout smolts hit the tideway they tend to tarry, moving backwards and forwards on every ebb and flow for a much longer period than their salmon counterparts.

After feeding and growing for 2–5 months, some of the smolts which descended in spring to the sea return in summer or autumn to the river. Here they are known by different

Arthur Oglesby

return as mature sea trout. Others, sadly, tend to regard sea trout merely as vermin. It is a sad fact that a river can only offer limited life-support systems. The man with his sights set on fishing for salmon, therefore, may consider sea trout as undesirable alien contenders, as mere juveniles, in a limited larder.

Sea trout—or salmon?

The anatomical differences between salmon and sea trout, although subtle, soon become evident. There is, of course, the undisputed scale count from the lateral line to the shoulder, but the tail is the main guide, and usually produces instant recognition. In salmon the tail is slightly forked and even when stretched still shows a concave shape. In sea trout the wrist of the tail is different and the tail itself is almost square or convex. All salmon may be picked up by the tail, but if an unidentified fish slides out of the hand it is a fair bet that it is a sea trout. To the trained eye, there are several other identifying factors, but for the novice the tail is the best guide.

Following a return of the young fish to the sea, many classic rivers will experience the first runs of mature sea trout. On the Spey, for instance, it is quite normal to find fresh sea trout as early as April. But the main runs may still be to come in May and June and it frequently happens that the bigger sea trout run the river earlier in the season. Not all these fish will be destined to spawn the following winter.

More nomadic than salmon

There is little doubt that most sea trout endeavour to spend some part of their year in freshwater. They are much more nomadic in their migrations than salmon. Indeed, only a very small percentage of salmon will ever make more than one freshwater migration. Many die as kelts and of those that do reach the sea again quickly, some fall to marine predators. Sea trout, however, have been known to migrate into freshwater as many as ten times, although there are few facts on the number of times successful spawning may take place.

names—finnock (and variants), whitling, herling, sewin, sprod, peal, among others— according to locality.

Why these small fish spend autumn and winter in their rivers of birth is not known. It is known that only few perform the reproductive act and that most come and go as the whim seizes them, either individually or in shoals; but that the longer they stay in freshwater the more their appearance and condition deteriorate. Many anglers seek them for sport and the table during early spring in the River Spey, for instance, which can be simply heaving with finnock up to the end of April. This seems to be the time when they make for the sea once more.

Finnock and herling

A usual weight for these fish is about 6–8oz, and so anglers may be forgiven for knocking them on the head. It is, however, difficult to establish the legality of this practice. Some anglers are of the opinion that the finnock, herling, or whatever, should be put back to migrate yet again to the sea, ultimately to

Sea trout

Mature sea trout weigh from 1lb to over 20lb but today it is quite an event to catch one over the 10lb mark. Scandinavia has produced some of the largest sea trout captured, while the Dovey in Wales has yielded at least two specimens of over 20lb. Until March 1969, the British rod-caught record was a fish of 22½lb caught by S R Dwight in 1946, coming from the River Frome in Dorset. Now, the record is open, with an acceptable minimum claim of 20lb.

Like salmon, the returning sea trout does not need to take food in freshwater, but, unlike salmon, does occasionally take food and seems to have a digestive mechanism adequate for this. But since sea trout do not seem to increase in length in freshwater, despite some feeding, they might be expected to suffer less from their stay there than salmon. The species, however, even maiden sea trout, do deteriorate after leaving the sea; and in many districts ripe fish at spawning lose as much weight for length as salmon.

Using up stored tissue and fat

There is little doubt, therefore, that the entire process of staying in freshwater calls upon the sea trout to use up much of its stored tissue and fat. Whatever food it might occasionally take, it certainly does not get sufficient to sustain it. Sea trout which have

Arthur Oglesby

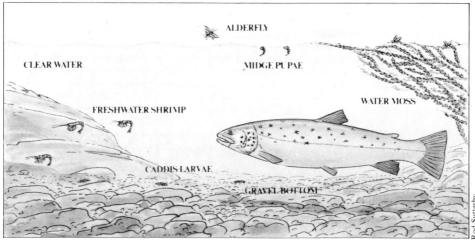

ALDERFLY

CLEAR WATER

MIDGE PUPAE

WATER MOSS

FRESHWATER SHRIMP

CADDIS LARVAE

GRAVEL BOTTOM

Rod Sutterby

run the river in April or May can be quite sorry-looking creatures by the end of September, and all sporting anglers will return such fish to the water with as little injury as possible.

On some rivers, of course, the sea trout do not begin to run until July or August. This can be a time when low water might frustrate easy passage up the river. In this respect sea trout are much more tenacious than salmon, and may frequently be seen moving through water barely sufficient to cover their backs.

Like salmon, the sea trout must have water of high purity. Sadly, suitable environments are continually being eroded and there are only a handful of worth while rivers in England today. Wales is better, but we look to Scotland for the majority of good rivers. Although more esteemed for its salmon fishing, the Spey is possibly the most prolific sea trout river in the United Kingdom. The Tweed gets good runs of big sea trout which few people ever seem to catch. The small rivers of the West Coast and the Isles abound with sea trout, but they are fickle and shy fish.

Superior to the salmon?

As a sporting fish, they are highly prized by anglers, many of whom are of the opinion that good sea trout are not only more sporting than salmon, but superior on the table. Unless the water is high and slightly coloured, the fish can be very difficult to catch in daylight. Night fishing with a fly is the epitome of sport, and on the classic streams it is the most practised method.

The sea trout, therefore, does not yet have to face the pressures now being made on salmon resources. With modest amounts of good husbandry, it seems to be a fish which can take reasonable care of itself, but it must never be seen casually as an indestructible resource. Unless something is done and done quickly, about the erosion of the suitable environment, the sea trout and the salmon may well pass into history as two of the greatest, but extinct, sporting fishes.

Arthur Oglesby

(Above left) Sea trout jumping, River Esk.
(Above) Dunbar Pool, on the Spey at Castle Grant.
(Left) The sea trout habitat is clear, pure water, fast and rich in small insects eaten when the fish is in the parr stage.
(Right) Natural food of the sea trout in freshwater is small insect life and crustaceans, while in the sea the species feeds on fish such as sandeel, pilchards and sprats.

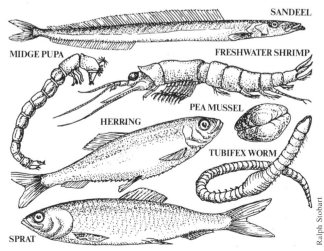

SANDEEL

MIDGE PUPA

FRESHWATER SHRIMP

PEA MUSSEL

HERRING

TUBIFEX WORM

SPRAT

Ralph Stobart

Trout rearing

During the early days of trout rearing, in the latter part of the 19th century, it was only the native brown trout which was reared, and all these were sold for restocking. Now, however, the accent is on the American rainbow trout because of its sporting qualities and the comparative ease with which it is reared. In recent times great advances have been made in the production of rainbow trout and in addition to restocking, the rainbow is becoming increasingly popular as a table fish.

The main difference between brown and rainbow trout, apart from their colour and shape, are growth rate, lifespan, and time of spawning. In the wild, native brown trout spawn during November, December or January, according to weather conditions and geographical location. There are two kinds of rainbow trout—one which spawns in the spring and one which spawns at about the same time as the brown trout. In captivity, rainbow trout can be induced to spawn at almost any time of year.

The methods of rearing trout are the same, irrespective of species, except that rainbow trout grow much more quickly than brown and have to be graded more often. They are not usually predatory when young, as are brown trout.

Conditions for breeding trout

Trout cannot be reared in any pit or pond, they must have an adequate supply of water of the correct chemical quality and temperature. It should be free from pollution, injurious metal salts with no silt or mud in suspension. Borehole water is usually preferred, but where river water has to be used, care must be taken to keep any silt away from eggs and young trout. Older fish are able to withstand a certain amount of mud or silt. The water used should be fully saturated with oxygen, and should be alkaline. A neutral pH value of between 7 and 8 is preferable, but slightly acidic water may be used if no other is available. The most suitable water temperature is about 15°C or slightly lower. Very cold water will put trout off the feed and high temperatures may kill them.

Important stages in the life of a trout are: the eyed egg, the alevin, the fry and the yearling. At each of these stages, trout require very precise water flows and temperature ranges.

Brood fish are usually kept in a special stewpond, and some time before they are fully ripe they are transferred to holding tanks where they can easily be removed for

(Below) Typical earth-banked stewponds for trout rearing. The water must be free from pollution, saturated with oxygen, alkaline. Ideal temperature is 15°C (59°F).

(Above) A circular fry tank at Packington Fisheries hatchery cleaned out and ready for use. The automatic fry feeder dispenses pellets at regular intervals.

spawning. Eggs from hen fish are stripped into a clean bowl containing no water and are afterwards fertilized, by introducing milt from male fish. Hen fish are usually completely stripped of their ova, then returned to another pond to recover. Male fish, however, may be used several times. After the milt has been added, the eggs are gently stirred and clean water is added to the bowl. After a while, the excess milt is washed away with successive changes of water and the eggs are placed in a receptacle and covered with water.

Hatching the eggs

The newly fertilized or 'green' eggs will noticeably swell. They are then transferred to incubators, remaining there until they hatch. Care must be taken to ensure that the water temperature does not fluctuate while the eggs are incubating, otherwise they will die. Any unfertilized eggs must be removed immediately and all through the incubation period dead eggs must be taken from the incubator trays. This is called 'egg-picking' and is one of the most important jobs in trout rearing, for if any eggs become infected with fungus, the infection will rapidly spread throughout the tray.

On hatching, the little trout, known as alevins, have a yolk-sac attached to the abdomen. They feed on this for some time, and when it has been used up the fish are termed 'ready to feed fry'. This 'swim-up' stage is a very critical one in trout rearing because it is sometimes difficult to get the fry to take food.

At the swim-up stage the fry are usually transferred to fry tanks, which may be rectangular or circular and are usually made of either plastic or concrete. The important thing is to ensure that the water velocity is not too great. Care must be taken to check the water temperature, pH, filters and screens regularly. Until the fry have settled down, these checks must be done several times a day; once the fry have adjusted to the new tanks the checks must be done at least once a day.

Eric Birch

In modern hatcheries fry are fed automatically with finely processed artificial food. Automatic feeders are made up of a hopper containing the food and a timing system which allows small quantities of food to fall on the water at regular intervals. It is essential to keep the fry tanks clear of faeces and uneaten food.

The fry remain in their tanks until they have outgrown them and then transferred to larger tanks or ponds. Here they may be fed either by hand or by machine. Automatic feeders used on ponds or larger tanks are much larger than those used on the fry tanks, but the system is the same. When the fry reach the yearling stage, they may be induced to use labour-saving devices known as 'self-feeders'.

These self-feeders may be mounted above tanks or allowed to float on specially designed, buoyant floats. This type of feeder relies on a pendulum positioned at one end in the food hopper, while the other protrudes into the water. Trout activate a nylon button at the end of the pendulum

(Above) Teeming trout fry in a circular tank. These small fish are fed either by hand or automatically. The water must be kept perfectly clean, clear of all uneaten food and well oxygenated. It is the most important aspect of trout rearing.
(Below) When they are large enough the trout are released into outdoor ponds. Here they can be fed by hand on pellets which supply a complete diet.

and food falls from the hooper into the water. This system avoids waste because the fish feed only when they are hungry.

Rainbow trout take more readily to self-feeders than brown trout and it is often necessary to feed the brown by hand or by automatic, pneumatic feeders which eject measured amounts of pellets at regular intervals.

Trout need protein, carbohydrates, minerals, fats and vitamins in their daily diet, and modern pellet feeds provide all that is necessary. Some pellets contain a very high proportion of protein, but for general restocking purposes about 40% is sufficient. All commercial pellet feeds are quite satisfactory and they are available in two main types. All fry pellets are of the sinking type, but for larger trout, floating pellets make the fish feed at the surface and it can easily be seen if the fish are taking their full ration.

The earth pond system

Many trout farms use the earth pond system which allows the trout to take a proportion of natural food. Snails, shrimps and other animals, such as caddis larvae, water beetles, midge larvae and those of pond and lake olives enter the ponds with the incoming water, particularly when this comes from a river or stream. This is an advantage because when the fish are released into angling waters they will be able to recognize their natural prey. If fed exclusively on pellets, they may take a little longer to become acclimatized to their new surroundings.

Any dead trout should be removed immediately from the stewpond or tank, otherwise fungus may spread through the whole stock. Healthy fish are able to throw off diseases, but the more they are crowded, the more likely they are to contract one of the many diseases to which they are susceptible.

Growth rates of brown and rainbow trout differ greatly. Browns grow comparatively slowly and continue to do so for 10 or more years in angling waters. But

Eric Birch

Hungry trout operating a Grice and Young pendulum feeder. This avoids food wastage for the feeder only releases food when the nylon button of the pendulum is nudged by the fish.

rainbows rarely live longer than five years, and in some waters the cocks do not survive their third year. This is due to their high metabolic rate: they use up all their energy during rapid growth. Without pushing them too much, brown trout can attain a size of 10in during their first year, though rainbows are able to grow to over 2½lb in the same period.

It is now possible to produce rainbow trout to double figure weights in two years by giving them plenty of space, an abundance of highly oxygenated water and as much food as they will eat. In ideal conditions they will eat at such a rate that their skin outgrow their scales and these stand out at right angles to their bodies for a short while.

The latest method of trout rearing is to employ floating cages in large lakes which solves the problem of eliminating waste products and also ensures an adequate supply of oxygen. Many fishing clubs and water authorities now employ this system because it is more efficient and cheaper than other methods.

Trout records

Stuart Linnell

A once-famous angling magazine, the 'Fishing Gazette', published between 1877-1966, contains many accounts of the capture of huge trout. On one occasion there was an upsurge of large estuarine 'bull' trout in Scotland (individual weights of more than 20 lb were claimed). Occasionally, giant migratory trout from the Kentish Stour were mentioned, the famous 'Fordwich Trout' of Izaak Walton's day. Between the two World Wars, a group of British fly fishermen discovered the huge sea-trout of Sweden's River Em, specimens of which exceeded 30 lb. New Zealand's Lake Taupo produced massive rainbows and even English chalk streams like the Kennet yielded the occasional trout of more than 10lb.

One thing in common

All these great trout had one thing in common: they had grown large by natural feeding. The migratory trout of the Stour and Em, for instance, fed on shoals of small fish in the shallow bays at the mouths of their parent rivers. The capture of such wild fish could be envied as an exceptional angling feat, as they required great angling skill.

A new development in trout fishing came with the establishment of the big reservoirs. When land is newly flooded the food is particularly rich, so trout grow quickly. But they are artificially introduced, and as the big lake settles down, the food supply diminishes

and competition with other species, notably coarse fish, increases. There is, therefore, a temptation to grow the fish to greater weights in breeding ponds before releasing them into the lake, in order to compensate for these two disadvantages. Even so, because the lakes are not often restocked, and because of the large unfished natural reserves of some lakes and the ability of the trout to spread out, there is still a degree of wildness in reservoir fish. The capture of large trout from such waters is a notable achievement.

But a more recent development in trout fishing is a cause of some disquiet so far as sporting standards are concerned. This has to do with the release of fish, which have already been raised to a large size by concentrated feeding techniques, into small areas of confined water. They do not have enough space to avoid being caught within a short time after their introduction, and the situation becomes ethically questionable when one reads descriptions of the techniques employed to catch them. It seems as if it hardly matters what fly is used if, only hours before, a human has been the source of a pellet shower.

So the angler has a moral problem; obviously he wants to catch these big fish, but at the same time, knowing the confrontation is rather artificial, he has to

(Left) Alan Pearson with the record rainbow trout. Caught in May 1977 at the Avington Fishery, Hants, it weighed 19½ It was taken with a Buff nymph on a size 10 hook and a 6lb b.s. leader. (Right) Netting a rainbow at Loch Avielochan, near Aviemore, in Scotland. The 15-acre loch is stocked every season with both brown and rainbow trout.

Bill Howes

convince himself that the apparently missing element of wildness is actually there. He also assumes that as not every fish can have come through the previous winter, those that did must have greater intelligence than other fish. But fish possess absolutely no intelligent reasoning powers, as any zoologist can prove. They do possess two qualities: an instinct for self-preservation in their native habitat, and the ability to be conditioned.

The justification?

The protection and food provided in the breeding ponds effectively conditions the fish to be more tame. Even though such fish are huge, the angler really knows that to hook one is a far less satisfying experience than that of a small boy who catches his first small roach or perch. So, to justify his action, the angler deceives himself and begins to believe in certain fallacies. One of these is that, when released, rainbow trout become wild almost immediately after having sampled a natural insect or two. Stocking a fishery himself, the author knows that, even as late as three weeks after their introduction, the stomachs of the trout are either empty or contain miscellaneous rubbish. The trout can be seen roaming around in shoals, desperately trying to find the daily ration of food pellets to which they were accustomed. Driven by sheer hunger, they will seize almost anything that moves,

be it an unrepresentative lure or a close imitation of a fly.

Friend—then enemy

It has been said that such fish, becoming wild almost immediately, recognise Man as an enemy. But perhaps only an hour or two before their release he has been the friendly provider of food! Newly released rainbows in chalk streams, where they can easily be seen, take up the most unprotected positions. It is some time before they react warily to people passing. Of course, many such fish are taken within minutes of stocking and are given neither time nor space to become natural feeders.

If you believed most anglers you would become convinced that every good fish taken had wintered through from the previous year, maybe with someone's fly in its mouth to prove it. But taking into account the lack of space and the weight of the fish, plus the short life span of the rainbow trout, most of these claims can be disproved.

The author's own experience highlights the truth that large rainbow trout, stocked in enormous numbers in small areas of water, are extremely easy to catch. A small chalk stream I fish in Normandy flows through a rainbow trout farm, the owner of which is successful in raising fish to great weights. Unfortunately, the bank of one of his pens broke down and a shoal of the bigger fish escaped into the river. I was dry fly fishing with a new, ultra-light carbon rod and spent a short time catching these fish. Every time a fly passed over, a fish took it. It was then just a question of time, with the rod bent almost to breaking point, to pull in the trout, unhook it and let it go. The pleasure soon palled, and we moved upstream to fish for the wild half-pound brown trout that the river produces. These 'brownies' are quite different from rainbows. They tend to live in the hardest places to fish, protected by stones or overhanging branches. They resist the 'wrong fly'. In short, they are a more challenging quarry than the largest rainbow.

Problem of perspective

It is difficult to place these new trout conditions into perspective. No criticism of those who grow the fish is implied, since trout fishing would simply not be available to most anglers if they were only able to fish for wild trout. The new trout also provide a new type of fishing which many people enjoy, even though it is expensive and less skilled than fishing for wild trout. But the automatic acceptance of such fish into the record lists should not be allowed. Press sensationalization of recent catches does nothing to inform the public. Because wild fish, similar in size, have been caught in the past, people simple assume that another big wild fish has been caught by an angler. They do not know what conditions were which enabled the angler to take it.

All record fish claims should arise from similar conditions, that is, a wild fish should be caught in its natural habitat. After all, no sea specimen hunter has the opportunity of seeking a cultured prey in an enclosed area. With very few exceptions, too, coarse fish are wild fish from wild places. Even reservoir trout have the opportunity for some natural growth, because of the infrequent stocking periods and wide dispersal areas.

The 'instant rainbow'

Fly fishing has developed as a sport dependent on a balanced mixture of physical and intellectual skills. Those who enjoy using these skills are now becoming dissatisfied with the growing artificiality of certain aspects of stillwater trout fishing. Although we have have not yet adopted the American term 'dude fishery' to describe fishing conditions, knowledgeable anglers are using their common sense and experience to put into perspective the record claims of captors of the 'instant rainbow'.

(Some years ago a situation arose concerning the brown trout. The record committee made a separate class of trout record, known as the 'cultivated' variety. As cultivated trout were hand-reared they would grow larger than wild fish. But the idea was dropped. Will this new development lead to a similar move? 'Wild' rainbow records could reflect the naturally growing fish, while the selectively bred giants would be listed separately. Editor.)

Fly fishing for trout has a pleasure all of its own. It is a combination of expertise and cunning, required at every stage of fishing, whether it is wet fly or dry fly. From casting and controlling the fly, to hooking and playing the fish, and finally landing it successfully, the angler must be always alert and match the legend of the trout as a furtive yet intelligent creature.

Ardea Photographics

Arthur Ogelsley

Salmon disease

The salmon population of our rivers is seriously affected at present by a widespread epidemic of a disease now known as ulcerative dermal necrosis (UDN). As the name implies, the disease causes ulcers in the skin which result in the tissue dying. Fish with UDN are recognized by the greyish-white patches of fungus which usually appear first on the head and afterwards along the back and sides of infected fish. The fungus is, however, a secondary infection which takes hold after the primary infection—probably a virus—has struck.

Secondary infection

To the average angler, fungus is just fungus, and there is a tendency to report that fish are suffering from UDN because of the outward appearance of patches of greyish-white growth. But there are many associated diseases that have similar symptoms- and have species of the common *Saprolegnia* fungus growth as a secondary infection. UDN is an ambiguous title given to an unspecified disease. It would be better called simply the 'salmon disease', and when the research workers have had another few years in which to experiment, we shall perhaps be given more specific titles for the various ulcerative fish diseases.

Salmon appear to contract UDN while out at sea, and it is only when they enter freshwater that the fungus, *Saprolegnia,* takes hold. The worst time for infection is during the colder months of autumn and spring, but, unfortunately, hot weather does nothing to 'burn out' an epidemic.

At first it was thought that the disease was caused by a bacteria called *Cytophaga columnaris,* since this was isolated from affected fish, but exhaustive tests did not confirm this and eventually the disease was given the name 'ulcerative dermal necrosis'.

It is the secondary infection that kills the fish, and not the disease itself. In the few instances where no secondary infection has occurred, affected fish have recovered.

On its own, scientists were unable to grow the unknown fungus found on affected fish,

(Left) The diseased patches on the snout of this salmon from the River Lune are typical of UDN. It is the head which develops those dirty white patches of fungus which eventually spread to the rest of the fish's body.
(Right) Again, it is the head of the fish which has been attacked. This brown trout has had the scores and fungus removed. While some coarse species, including roach, seem to be affected it is not yet certain whether UDN is responsible or a related form of it can attack coarse species.

Arthur Oglesby

but it readily grew in association with *Cytophaga columnaris*. This suggested that the disease may be the result of an association of two organisms and not a single one as previously thought.

Research has produced a great deal of evidence to suggest that UDN is infectious, but so far there is no firm scientific proof. One fact has emerged out of all the research: the current outbreak did not spread by infection but was rather a simultaneous outbreak in many places.

UDN epidemic

The present epidemic of UDN began in the south and south-west of Ireland during the autumn of 1964. In the spring of 1966 it appeared in English salmon rivers and was later confirmed in Welsh and Scottish game fishing rivers.

The disease spread rapidly, and in 1968 outbreaks among mature trout were confirmed in many reservoir fisheries, some of which were fed from rivers where UDN occurred. But other fisheries had no direct link with affected waters. UDN was confirmed in Germany during 1972 and, in 1976, broke out in the Baltic, affecting salmon and sea trout. Also in 1976

a report from Scandinavia stated that an outbreak of what appeared to be UDN was affecting grayling, huchen (Danube salmon), brown and brook trout, pike and whitefish. Starting in spring, it quickly spread.

When it became obvious that the disease might become a serious threat to game fish all over the British Isles, steps were taken to try to restrict its spread by encouraging anglers to disinfect tackle, clothing and boats, although no one quite knew what they were trying to protect against. Serious attempts to contain the disease gradually diminished as the spread continued. Anglers had to live with the fact that UDN was here and it looked like staying for some time.

The immense losses of salmon from UDN do not seem to have placed the species in danger of extinction, because infected fish have been able to spawn successfully, even though research suggests that the mortality rate of salmon from infected parents is much greater than those of clean fish.

Apparently UDN does not affect coarse fish, and yet coarse fish stocks, particularly perch, have been severely affected by a similar disease. Roach have also suffered losses and the cause still remains a mystery.

Eric Birch

Salmon rods

Salmon rods may be divided into two main types—spinning rods (sometimes known as bait casting rods) and fly rods.

Spinning rods

Spinning rods, the kind more widely used for salmon fishing, are usually 8–10ft in length. For rivers requiring the use of heavy baits and lines with high b.s., that is, over 15lb, a double-handed rod of 9½–10ft, used with a multiplier reel, is the best type. This combination gives good control of the bait and will handle big fish in the larger, stronger rivers such as the Hampshire Avon and the Wye. It is also suitable for fishing with a prawn bait.

Smaller rivers, where lighter lines and bait may be used, call for a shorter rod, 8½–9ft long, used with a fixed-spool or multiplier style reel. Line of 10–15lb and casting weight of up to 1oz are suited to use with this combination. This outfit can be used for worming for salmon, although a longer rod is probably preferable.

Ideally, a salmon spinning rod is strong, with a medium-to-stiff action. The through action favoured in the past to assist in avoiding casting problems, such as overruns by the multiplier reel, is no longer essential as reel design has improved. The newer kind of action is preferable, even for use with the multiplier.

Rod making materials

Spinning rods can be made from any of the usual rod-making materials—carbon-fibre, tubular and solid glass-fibre, and built cane. The best materials are either carbon-fibre or

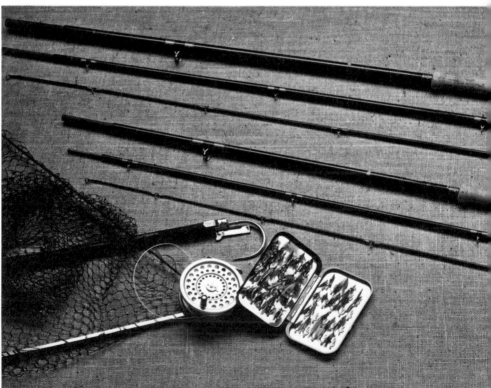

Irish Tourist Board

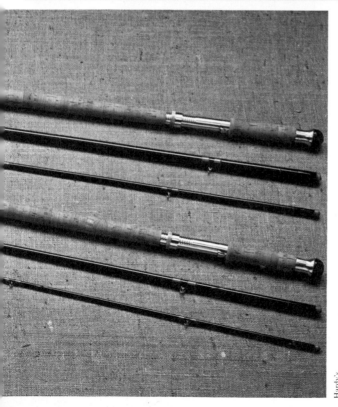

Hardy's

(Above) A prime Irish salmon spinning and fixed-spool combination. Double-handed salmon spinning rods are longer and stronger than coarse spinning rods. They need to have sliding or fixed-screw winch fittings for reel seating and be able to control strong-fighting salmon in large, swift-flowing rivers. Some salmon spinning rods are used with multipliers which sit on top, because thumb pressure is used to control spool spin, so rod ring position is important.

(Left) The salmon fly rod can also be used double-handed. These models are Hardy Fibalite hollow fibre glass rods of 12½ft and 14ft. Of 14¾oz and 16oz, they show screw grip reel fittings.

Salmon rods

(Left) In terms of salmon rods, this spinning outfit, in use at Ballynahinch, Co Galway, is quite short. It would be difficult to control a large salmon with this rod.

(Right) The angler here is holding the rod well up in order to keep in touch with his fish. Any slackness of line at this stage could lead to the fish jumping off the hook and being lost.

(Far right) Having beached his salmon, caught from the Lune at Newton, Don Oliver is using the correct tailing grip to pick the fish up.

Irish Tourist Board

tubular glass. Solid glass-fibre is strong but is not pleasant to use due to its weight and action, while built cane is no longer in common use.

Two-piece construction, with glass spiggot joints in the case of carbon-fibre and tubular glass, is standard in salmon spinning rods. Handles are usually of cork, with either sliding fittings or a fixed screw winch fitting to hold the reel. Stainless steel rod rings are the most commonly used. These have a hard chrome finish to withstand wear from the line. The rod should have enough rings to ensure that the strain on the line is distributed evenly along the rod's length. On rods used with the multiplier style of reel, which sits on top, the rings need to be carefully positioned to avoid contact between line and rod.

Basic outfit

A basic outfit for spinning for salmon comprises a rod of 9–9½ft and a fixed spool or multiplying reel capable of carrying at least 100 yards of 15lb b.s. line. The reel should be held, for preference, by a screw winch fitting. This should be situated 18–20in from the bottom end of the rod with a multiplying reel.

Built-cane spinning rods are seldom seen nowadays but were very popular before the advent of tubular glass and carbon-fibre. Some are manufactured today, mainly longer models of 9–10ft, usually teamed with a multiplier reel, but they are being superceded by carbon-fibre rods.

Fly rods

Salmon fly rods are designed for use by one or two hands, according to the style of casting employed. The double-handed variety are usually 12–14ft long, certainly over 11ft. The ideal length for an all-round rod is 12½–13ft, and this, coupled with a double tapered size 9 line, is suitable for fishing most of the salmon waters in this country.

The principal materials used for salmon fly rods are built-cane, tubular glass-fibre, carbon-fibre, and greenheart, which is a hard but pliant wood. Many salmon fishermen prefer a rod of built-cane, particularly a model with spliced joints. These, so called because the sections are spliced together with a binding tape, form a very strong joint. The spliced joint is of great value in Spey casting, a form of roll cast employed when obstructions behind the angler prevent a normal back cast. The Spey style exerts a

44

Arthur Oglesby

twisting force along the rod but spliced joints resist the tendency of the rod's sections to twist at the joints and so lose alignment.

The relatively new carbon-fibre fly rods, although still expensive, have several advantages and are increasingly popular. Apart from casting as well as a top-quality built-cane model, they have the valuable assets of lightness and strength, and so may be used, where necessary, in greater lengths without any strain on the angler. Their small diameter is a great advantage in windy conditions, where the thicker built-cane rod would offer more wind resistance.

Tubular glass is the most common material for this type of rod for, apart from giving a serviceable rod, it is much cheaper than either carbon-fibre or built-cane. Although heavier than carbon-fibre, the tubular glass rod has the advantage of lightness over the built-cane variety. A $12\frac{1}{2}$–13ft model makes a good all-round rod for salmon fly fishing.

Action

Most salmon fly rods today have an action that may be felt right through from the heavy tip to the butt. A tip with this fairly rigid action is required because of the need to 'mend' the line or straighten it out. This need arises when the strength of the current varies at different points across the stream and the line is pulled into a bow shape as it is carried downstream. This in turn carries the fly back across the flow at an unnatural angle, making it unacceptable to the salmon. The fisherman must then roll the line to 'mend' it as the bow shape not only presents the fly unfavourably but also lessens the effectiveness of a strike should there be, by an odd chance, a take. A heavy tipped rod enables a weighty length of double tapered line to be lifted off the water and 'mended' with reasonable ease.

Single-handed fly rods of $9\frac{1}{2}$ft or longer are suited to fishing for salmon in small to medium sized rivers, where smaller flies are used. They should not be used, though, to lift long lines, as this subjects them, and the angler's arm, to considerable strain. Fishing in these conditions requires a light, 10ft rod of carbon-fibre, tubular glass or built-cane, equipped with a double tapered line, size 7, on a reel large enough to take 100 yards of 15lb b.s. backing line. This outfit should prove equal to the salmon encountered in the smaller waters.

Reservoir rods

The purpose of a rod in any type of fishing is to act as a guide for the line and as a spring to absorb the effects of hard-fighting fish. But in fly fishing the rod must also be supple enough throughout all, or part of its length to cast a fly which is virtually weightless. The line is weighted according to the type of fishing it is designed for and so rods will differ according to the weight of line they can carry. Rods also have different actions and, with the introduction of newer materials, there is variation of construction as well.

Split-cane

Wood has always been considered the best material for fly-rod construction. The peak of wooden fishing rod construction is split-cane, which tends to have an 'all-through' action which means that the full length of the rod will be involved when playing a fish or casting. But split-cane has drawbacks in its maintenance and in its casting ability. Split-cane cannot be stored even slightly wet because it will quickly warp and rot. The problem with its action is that when used for casting long distances it can take on a permanent curve, called a 'set'. But its greatest drawback is its weight when compared with today's man-made materials.

Glassfibre

From split cane, with its inherent disadvantages, came the development of glass-fibre rods from the US. Glass-fibre is less expensive than split cane; it is also lighter and requires less maintenance. But again it will take on a 'set' if grossly abused, although not as badly as will split cane.

During the 20-odd years since it was introduced, glass-fibre has progressed from the solid section to 'hollow glass'. The great advantage of hollow glass-fibre rods is that they can be tailored to give any kind of action to suit individual preference. Some anglers prefer to use nymphs to tempt fish rising to the surface and would probably choose a double-taper line. Consequently a

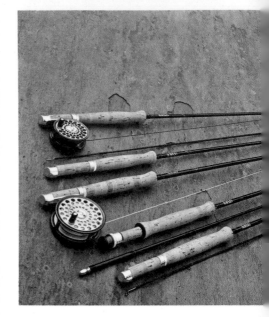

Carbon-fibre fly rods. The Farnborough, for reservoirs, is second from bottom.

rod with a through action will be preferred. For reservoir fishing, with the huge areas of water, long casting is essential and so, coupled with a heavy line, a rod with a tip-action will be the choice. Some reservoir anglers prefer through-action rods, but a rod with the action in its top part tends to be more powerful, propelling the line farther.

Carbon-fibre

Glass-fibre rods have now probably reached their peak in casting performance, but there is now a new material which has as good a casting action. This is carbon-fibre, another development from the US, first introduced into Great Britain about three years ago.

The material has all the advantages of glass-fibre but is much lighter, and has a smaller diameter for the same power. There is one big difference—carbon-fibre rods are

Split-cane

Hollow-glass

Carbon-fibre

Hardy

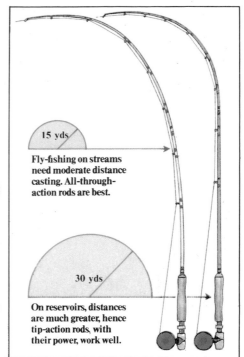

15 yds

Fly-fishing on streams
need moderate distance
casting. All-through-
action rods are best.

30 yds

On reservoirs, distances
are much greater, hence
tip-action rods, with
their power, work well.

Rod Sutterby

much more expensive than all the others. Carbon-fibre was originally seen as a short, very light fishing rod. Now a number of tackle manufacturers are offering their brands of carbon-fibre rods in lengths between 7 ft and 10 ft 6 in for trout fishing.

The selection of a rod must take into account the use to which it will be put, and the type of water to be fished. One can then chose between split-cane, glass-fibre or carbon-fibre.

Reservoir rods

Reservoir fishing has become an important part of game fishing. Large numbers of anglers fish these waters from the banks and from boats. This type of fishing demands distance-casting and continual retrieval of the line. This means the rod will be in constant use, so the angler must choose a rod which will enable him to cast efficiently into the high winds often present on reservoirs, without becoming too tired to fish.

The rod, therefore, should be as powerful and as light as possible, so split cane is clearly

unsuitable. This leaves a choice between glass-fibre and carbon-fibre.

A carbon rod will do all the things that a glass-fibre rod can do. But it will not cast farther and will not improve an angler's skill at fly casting. The advantage of this material is that less effort is needed in casting, partly because there is more 'power' in the carbon-fibre sections from which the rod was made, and partly because the smaller diameter of the rod creates less air resistance.

Cost is a factor we all have to bear in mind. At present carbon-fibre rods are expensive, but because inferior carbon-fibre is worse than inferior glass-fibre, selection must not be based purely on cheapness. Your selection of a reservoir rod must be based on sound advice from the dealer, your experience and judgement of the rods you are offered, and the style of fishing which you intend to do with it. A good rod will last a lifetime and there can be nothing worse than trying to use unsuitable equipment. It is a false economy to buy cheap tackle.

Arthur Ogelsley

Brook rods

Fly fishing in brooks and small rivers places a premium on accurate casting at short range. This is the basis of all brook fishing, but when selecting your rod it is important to consider the differences between brooks.

A brook running over flat country, or, if on hilly ground, with low banks, can be fished best with a short flexible rod. The shorter the rod (within reason) the more line will be in the air when casting, flexing the rod better and producing greater casting accuracy. A good choice would be a $6\frac{1}{2}$-$7\frac{1}{2}$ft rod, designed to carry a No. 4 or No. 5 line.

This is the kind of rod usually recommended for fishing small rivers and brooks, but on water with either high, steep banks, or trees and bushes that impede the back-cast it may impose a severe handicap.

In such circumstances it may be preferable to use a much longer rod of 9ft or so, to keep the back-cast above the obstructions, or, if it is flexible as it ought to be, to permit easy, accurate casting where no back-cast is possible, however high the line is thrown.

Matters are sometimes complicated by the fact that quite small brooks, capable of naturally producing trout of only modest size, are nowadays stocked with much bigger fish. No great problem exists if the banks are clear and the stream is relatively free from obstructions, but if there are bridges, culverts and bankside trees or bushes which prevent the angler from following a hooked fish up and down the stream, then stronger tackle will be necessary.

This tackle includes a more powerful rod, which, in conjunction with a strong leader, allows the angler to put more pressure on a big fish, stopping it before it goes through a culvert, or too far past a bankside tree, beyond which the angler cannot follow.

Heavy line

This poses a problem; the powerful rod is less able to throw an accurate short line. Some compromise is necessary. This involves using a heavier fly line than would normally be chosen to fish a small water in order to flex the more powerful rod, and also choosing a rod in a material that is more tolerant of under-loading. Split cane and carbon-fibre fall into this category, fibreglass does not.

Some small streams run through tunnels of trees and can only be fished by wading, using a very short rod. In this situation it is best to use the top section of a 9ft split cane rod plugged into a separate handle, making a rod with a total length of about $5\frac{1}{2}$ft.

Other brooks are so narrow that, except in a few places, casting is impossible and all the angler can do is to lower a fly straight down or, if he uses a leaded pattern, swing it like a

A small stream, the River Teise, in Kent. On this day there had been a drop in water level, giving very coloured conditions. So well-known all-rounder Geoffrey Bucknall is using the wet fly fished just below the surface on a slow-sinking line. The trout from this rich little brook come well if they reach a pound in weight.

Bill Howes

pendulum to the place where he wants it to drop. Paradoxically, this calls for quite a long rod, 9ft at least, and preferably longer still, to allow the angler to keep well back from the water and avoid scaring the trout. In such waters it is necessary to use quite a short leader, often as short as 3-4ft, otherwise the weight of the fly line will pull the fly up to the tip ring of the rod directly it is released. In places where the brook widens and proper casting is possible, the leader can be lengthened to the usual 6-7½ft.

Dense bushes

On a stream with very dense bushes, where fishing is only possible by poking the rod through branches and lowering the fly, the only answer is to use the longer rod and a level nylon monofilament leader approximately twice as long as the rod. This allows a leader fly to be drawn up to within ½in of the tip ring while the rod is pushed through the branches, after which the nylon is paid out, allowing the fly to fall into the water.

Before embarking upon this procedure, it is sensible to decide how a fish is to be landed if one is hooked. If it is small enough, it can be hauled up to the tip ring, but if it is too big for that, a landing net will be necessary and unless it can be worked through the jungle to where the trout can be netted, the whole operation is impossible to bring to a satisfactory conclusion.

Whatever kind of brook one intends to fish, it will almost certainly include at least some parts where, for one reason or another, a normal overhead cast cannot be made. The chosen rod should therefore be capable of roll-casting easily and accurately. If it will not, it will prove a handicap to some extent on almost every water, and on some it will be almost useless.

It has to be remembered that it takes time and practice to obtain the best results from any rod. The fly fisherman whose experience has been confined to reservoirs, lakes and larger rivers where long casting is necessary, should practise with his brook tackle until he can roll-cast, throw a very high back-cast into a convenient gap and pull out a forward

cast at an angle to it, and even cast a line with a curve in it to put a fly round a corner.

When fishing small streams, the rod will often be nearer to the fish than in any other kind of fly fishing, so it is as well to avoid white or yellowish rods, and to remove the shine from others, either by rubbing the high-gloss varnish down with oil and pumice powder or applying an extra coat of matt varnish.

To sum up, there is no ideal rod for every sort of brook. You have to pick one, or perhaps more, to suit the water or waters you intend to fish. Do not make the mistake of thinking that cheap, poor-quality tackle is suitable for little waters. In fact, these are more demanding of quality and above all, versatility, than any other trout water.

Ken Whitehead

Hardy Bros.

(Above) An angler worm-fishing on the River Towy, in Wales. Perhaps it does qualify for a better title than stream, but its pure, tumbling shallows offer the same attractions.
(Right) A brook rod, 6ft long and weighing $2\frac{1}{2}$ oz. It is manufactured from Palakona split cane.
(Far right) This 6ft 3in fly rod, in hollow glass fibre, weighs 2 oz. It is designed for fishing tiny streams, and burns with the smallest flies.

Fly reels

While all anglers agree that a casting reel must be properly designed if it is to work efficiently, many feel that the fly reel is a very unimportant tackle item. This may be because in fly fishing the reel has no influence on the cast, whereas when spinning the reel has a dominant effect on distance. But the fly reel is an item which warrants careful thought, because a fly reel often does more than a fixed-spool when playing a fish.

There are several reasons for this, and one is the faster runs made by game fish when compared with most coarse and saltwater species. Fly lines are thicker than monofilament so a fly reel empties quickly and as the line pile gets smaller so the spool turns faster. Under these circumstances, if the spool is a poor fit within the reel frame it will jam and the fish will be lost.

Three basic types of fly reel

Fly reels form three basic types: the single-action type where the drum moves one revolution for every turn of the handle (on a well-filled trout reel this recovers approximately 8in of line); the multiplier type where the drum performs perhaps two revolutions (thereby recovering approximately 16in of line) for every turn of the handle, and the clockwork or automatic type where the spool is driven by a spring. This spring winds itself up when you take line from the reel.

The basic function of any reel is to hold a sufficient quantity of line for the type of fishing being practised. Because fly fishing is not all the same, an angler practising one method of fishing may have a different reel requirement to another. Any of the three different types will cover all methods (providing the size, and therefore the line capacity, is right) but some methods may not fully utilize all the advantages of the more sophisticated reels. An angler fishing another method would be helped considerably by these additional features.

To illustrate this, imagine an angler fishing

(Above) Two single-action fly reels, the Hardy Husky and Perfect models. The Perfect has the ball-bearing race and check and regulator mechanism exposed.
(Right) Basically, the fly reel must carry enough line for the angler to hook and play his fish. Reels in the Hardy Lightweight range are shown here.

wet fly downstream on a small brook, where the trout average 8oz and where the record for the water is under 1lb. The angler makes short casts. He carries little slack in his hand and there is no need to give line when a fish is being played. Clearly, such a situation imposes minimal demands upon the reel.

A simple, single-action model will do all that is needed, for the reel does little beyond serving as a convenient line store. The multiplier and the automatic would also be suitable but in the situation described their more sophisticated features would not be fully used.

Problems on chalk streams

Now let us imagine a different situation. Our angler is fishing a dry fly on a southern chalk stream. The distances he will cast will be greater and sometimes he will switch quickly from short to long. Because he is casting upstream he will often have a lot of slack

52

Fly reels

line. The size of the fish varies from an average of 1lb, but there is a good chance of a three or even a five-pounder. Due to the clear water a fine leader is used, so when a hooked fish makes long runs our angler sometimes has to follow.

Advantage of the multiplier

Again the single-action reel could deal with this but anglers find that in this setting the quicker recovery afforded by a multiplier is an advantage. Other anglers may find that an automatic reel gives them still more advantages, for the automatic recovers line even faster than a multiplier. Close control can be vital, particularly when you have to get up off your knees, quickly wind up the slack and then follow a big fish down river.

Now visualize an angler wading the shore line of a large reservoir. He is casting about 25 yards and working his flies back by bunching the line in his left hand. When the flies are two-thirds of the way back a fish takes. The angler wants to get the fish under proper control as quickly as he can but has about 16 yards of slack line to deal with.

Again the single-action reel will cope but it will take so long to wind up the slack (over 60 turns) that some anglers ignore the reel completely and resort to stripping in the line to try to keep in touch with their fish. Many highly experienced anglers find this less than satisfactory, and again use either a multiplier or an automatic to wind up the slack to get them more quickly into tight-line control.

The reel's important function

These examples show the very different settings which exist in trout fly fishing. There are lots of others, but those described show not only that the reel has an important function, but also how the requirement varies.

The average single-action reel is around $3\frac{1}{2}$in in diameter. With the aim of getting the fastest possible recovery, the spool is sometimes so narrow that you cannot get your finger between the flanges to control the spool when the fish runs. This can be a problem and is something to watch out for. To overcome this the spool edge is

Garcia Mitchell

(*Above*) *In controlling a fish of this size the angler may need a reel that allows a quick recovery of line, but this single-action reel has done the job.*
(*Above right*) *The Hardy Flyweight takes a DT-4-F with no backing.*
(*Below*) *An advanced fly reel, the Garcia-Mitchell 710 Automatic, which takes a WF-6-F and 70 yards of backing.*

Garcia Mitchell

Hardy's

sometimes swept up and over the outer edge of the reel frame. This 'exposed rim' makes a readily accessible braking surface but it is not without hazards.

The rim is vulnerable to bangs and knocks (aluminium is a soft material and dents easily). If the rim gets distorted it can bind on the frame and the reel will jam. Equally, the 'wrap over' flange is a trap for dirt and grit. One grain can make the reel stick.

The design of the multiplying fly reel is virtually the same as the single-action, except that the handle is not fastened direct to the spool but is connected by a train of gears. These gears impart the multiplying action where one turn of the handle drives the spool round more than once.

Advantage of high gear-ratio

To get the quickest possible recovery a high gear ratio would seem to offer the best advantage, but beware of reels that are over-geared. The highest practicable ratio is less than 2:1 for when you go higher (faster) the gears work against the angler to such a degree that it becomes almost impossible to turn the handle.

Most single-action and multiplying fly reels have a permanent click-check to stop the spool over-running. On the best reels the tension of this check is adjustable to suit the breaking strain of the leader being used. The adjustment is made either by a milled screw, an adjustment cam, or by moving the click spring across an adjusting rack. Each method works equally well. Another feature found on better-grade reels is the facility to change spools quickly, so affording the opportunity to switch lines (floating/sinking, and so on).

The automatic reel

The automatic reel has no handle and line is recovered by a spring. The spring is wound by the action of pulling line from the reel. When the angler wants to recover line he releases a trigger and the line is rapidly wound back (20 yards is rewound in approximately five seconds). Some anglers find the extra weight of the automatic a disadvantage, but the enthusiastic user will tell you that the greater control he has over hooked fish more than compensates for the extra weight.

Care is needed when purchasing an automatic as some of the reels available are too small and will barely handle the most popular size lines in use today. They accept a size 4 but will not handle a double taper 6 plus a reasonable quantity of backing. Again, make sure that you choose a reel with the facility to change the spool. This gives

Fly reels

(Above) The Hardy Viscount 150 mounted on a Bruce and Walker salmon rod.
(Right) A Japanese fly reel, the Diawa 734, which can carry line up to AFMTA 9 (see Part 7, 'Fly Lines').
(Below right) The Abu Delta distinctively shaped fly reels have oval stripping bars that help avoid line wear.

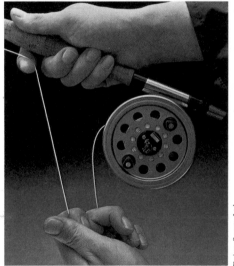

you all the advantages of having several reels when you want to switch from one type of line to another.

Any fly reel, whether it is a single-action, a multiplier or an automatic, should be fitted with a well-designed guard. Without this, the action of stripping out line will quickly wear a groove in the reel frame and soon both the reel and the line will be damaged.

There are so few moving parts in a fly reel that maintenance is hardly worth mentioning. An occasional spot of oil on the spool spindle takes care of the revolving parts and a liberal smear of grease on the check pawl is all that is needed. With the automatic, follow the maker's instructions regarding oiling.

Beware of dismantling the re-wind mechanism because if the spring is disturbed getting it back can be tricky. Better to leave it alone and let the maker's own Service Centre check it over every two or three years.

Bill Howes

Daiwa Sports Ltd

Bill Howes

Arthur Ogelsley

Fly lines

In the early days of fly fishing, lines were made of plaited horsehair. This was later replaced by a mixture of horsehair and silk, then by pure silk, plaited, tapered and dressed (impregnated and coated) with linseed oil.

The oil-dressed silk line was in universal use for three-quarters of a century, until it was replaced by the modern plastic-coated fly lines which consist of a plaited dacron core with a coating of polyvinyl chloride (PVC). For sinking fly lines, the PVC is impregnated with powdered metal, the quantity used determining the rate at which the line sinks.

Plasticizer

PVC is a hard material unless it contains a suitable 'plasticizer', which is introduced during manufacture. With time this is lost from the line, which then becomes hard and cracks. The loss of plasticizer is accelerated by heat and by greasing the line. Fortunately it can be restored by the use of special replasticizing grease such as 'Permaflex'.

A wide variety of line is now available, identified by a code known as the AFTM (American Federation of Tackle Manufacturers) system. This code tells you the kind of taper the line has, the weight of the first 30ft of the line, and whether the line is a floating or a sinking one.

So-called 'level lines' are of the same thickness all along their length; they are little used and their only merit is that they are cheap. They are designated by the letter L.

Double taper lines

'Double taper lines', designated DT, have both their ends tapered for more than 10-12ft, giving a fine end which falls more lightly on the water. The idea of a double taper is that when one end is worn, you can reverse the line on your reel and use the other end. These lines are usually 90ft long.

'Forward taper lines', otherwise known as 'weight-forward' (WF) resemble the first 30ft or so of a double taper with 40ft of very fine fly line attached. (In fact there is no actual attachment, both core and coating are continuous.) This allows more line to be 'shot' through the rings when casting. Recently, lines have been introduced with the first, heavier part longer than 30ft. These are called 'long belly lines'.

'Shooting heads' are similar in principle to 'forward taper lines', but instead of the fine shooting line being a continuation of the

Line Coding—Association of Fishing Tackle Manufacturers

Number	Weight (in Grains)	
1	60 (54–66)	**Abbreviations**
2	80 (74–86)	L =Level Line
3	100 (94–106)	DT =Double Taper
4	120 (114–126)	WF =Weight Forward
5	140 (134–146)	ST =Shooting Taper (or head)
6	160 (152–168)	F =Floating
7	185 (177–193)	F/S =Fast sinking, wet tip
8	210 (202–218)	VFS =Very fast sinking
9	240 (230–250)	
10	280 (270–290)	**Examples**
11	330 (318–342)	ST–8–S =Shooting head No 8 Sinking
12	380 (368–392)	DT–6–F =Double Taper No 6 Floating

(Left) The AFTM coding for fly lines classifies lines according to weight, while abbreviations either side describe their type and performance.

(Right) When accuracy is demanded the double taper (A) is most suitable, while the forward taper (B) allows the angler to cast into wind. The shooting head (C) gives long-distance casting. Sinking lines (at foot) give varying sinking rates.

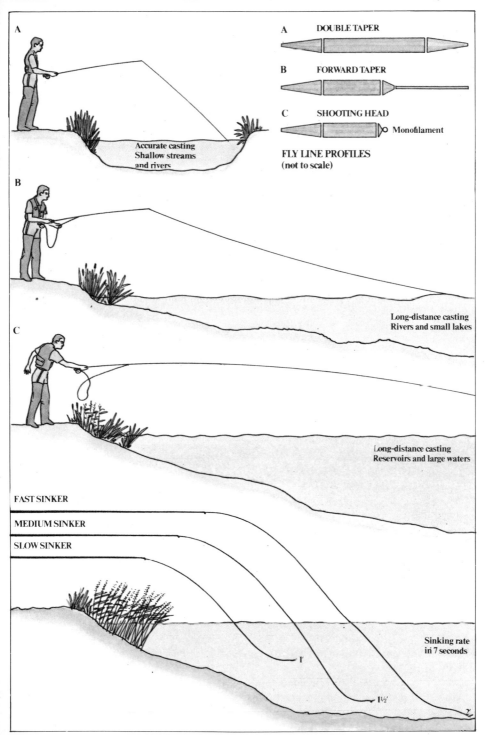

A

DOUBLE TAPER

B

FORWARD TAPER

C

SHOOTING HEAD

Monofilament

FLY LINE PROFILES
(not to scale)

A

Accurate casting
Shallow streams
and rivers

B

Long-distance casting
Rivers and small lakes

C

Long-distance casting
Reservoirs and large waters

FAST SINKER

MEDIUM SINKER

SLOW SINKER

Sinking rate
in 7 seconds

1'

1½'

2'

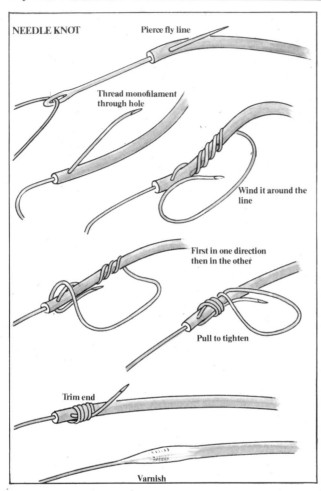

NEEDLE KNOT

Pierce fly line

Thread monofilament through hole

Wind it around the line

First in one direction then in the other

Pull to tighten

Trim end

Varnish

Knots in fly lines must not impede the passage of the line through the rod rings. Use the Needle knot (left) to join the line to the backing and the Double Grinner (right) to link the fly line with the leader.

PVC-coated fly line, it consists of nylon monofilament attached to the fly line by a special knot. This allows even more line to be 'shot' in casting, and as the fly line is usually cut from a 'double taper', shooting heads are much cheaper than either 'double' or 'forward taper lines'.

Shooting heads

Good tackle shops will usually sell halves of 'double tapers' for making shooting heads, which will need a further reduction in length, usually to 30-36ft.

All these lines can be of various floating or sinking qualities. There are floaters, slow sinkers, medium sinkers and fast sinkers, as well as floating lines with sinking tips. They are all available in a range of weights, numbered 3 to 12. The more powerful your rod, the heavier the line it will need.

Let us look at some examples of coding. A line coded DT7F is a double-tapered floating line, weight No. 7. A WF9S is a forward taper sinking line, weight No. 9 and so on.

The reason why the weight number refers to the first 30ft or so of the line, is that 30ft is about as much as an average fly caster can control when he whips the line back and forth in false-casting. Good casters can handle more, but in practical fishing there is no advantage in having more than about 45ft, which only very good casters can handle.

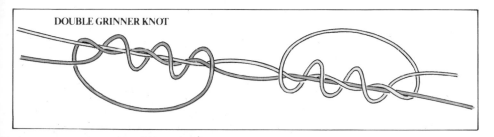

DOUBLE GRINNER KNOT

Bill Howes

When you buy a rod you will find that its maker has specified what size line it will carry. Remember that this refers to 30ft of line in the air. If your rod has a recommendation of No. 7 line, that means it will work nicely when you are switching 30ft of line in the air.

Short casting

If the kind of fishing you do involves mainly short casting, and you will seldom have more than 24ft or so in the air, you will do better with the heavier No. 8 line. If, on the other hand, you often put 35ft or more into the air, then you should use a lighter line.

For dry fly and nymph fishing, floating lines are used; the sinking lines are mainly for lake and reservoir fishing when wet flies and lures of various kinds are needed. Slow sinkers sink at a rate of about 1ft in 7 seconds; medium sinkers 1ft in 5 seconds; fast sinkers, or as they are sometimes called, 'Hi-D' lines sink at about 1ft in 3 seconds. By counting the seconds after casting, you can decide how deep you allow your line to sink before starting the retrieve.

Backing line

For most kinds of fly fishing, your fly line needs backing; that is, some monofilament or braided, uncoated line is wound on to the reel first, and then the coated fly line is attached to it. Flattened monofilament of about 25lb b.s., or special monofilament sold for backing purposes, is cheaper than braided backing line, and easier to connect securely to the coated fly line.

Monofilament backing line is attached to the fly line with a needle-knot. The same knot can be used to tie a short piece of ordinary round-section monofilament to the other end of the fly line, to which in turn the tapered leader (cast) is knotted with a three-turn blood knot or a Double Grinner knot. All these knots are very secure, and have the advantage of being able to pass easily through the rod rings.

The pale-coloured lines are easier to see against dark reflections but harder to see against a ripple or a bright reflection. In certain conditions, such as in bright sunshine or against a dark background of rocks or trees, pale lines being false-casts in the air can scare fish. When lying on the water's surface all lines viewed from below look dark, regardless of their actual colour.

Fly lines are expensive, so it is sensible to take good care of them.

Wet fly lines

In the days when the only fly lines available to the game fisherman were of dressed silk, considerable time and trouble had to be expended to maintain or renew the oils and soft substances used in the dressing to ensure that the line remained waterproof and would continue to float on every outing.

This was particularly important for the correct presentation of the floating fly—the order of the day on very many fisheries, particularly the Southern chalk streams. In other parts of the country, fishing a sunken fly was perfectly acceptable, and many anglers discovered that they could work their sunken flies more effectively if the line dressing wore off, resulting in a waterlogging of the line and so, slow sinking.

Plastic-coated fly lines

In recent years the development of plastic-coated fly lines has proceeded apace, offering the angler a very wide choice of line profiles at varying densities. These have enabled him to fish efficiently in any water, no matter at what depth the trout (or salmon) might be feeding. The selection of the correct line profile is dictated by necessity. Where casting range is short, and delicacy and accuracy essential, the correct choice will be the double taper profile or the single taper lines offered by some manufacturers. After all, if one is talking about casting a maximum distance of some 15 yards, there seems little point in loading with a line twice that length.

The use of half a double taper line, attached to a backing of nylon monofilament or braided Terylene, reduces the size of reel needed, which, in turn, reduces the weight at the butt end of the rod, leading to more efficient and comfortable casting. It should not be overlooked that half a fly line costs proportionately less than a full one, whether one purchases from a cooperative dealer, or simply buys a full line and shares it with a friend.

Where longer casting is required, or the water is very deep or fast moving, the forward taper line is preferable. This has the casting weight at the forward end—hence the name—while the rest of the length is made up of fine 'running line'. Forward taper lines vary in length, ranging from the 30 yard standard up to 40 yards or more.

The shooting head

The shooting head is simply a variation upon the forward taper theme, whereby the actual fly line is restricted in length to that needed to give the rod the correct action— usually 7-12 yards. This short section is spliced to the backing line, generally of nylon monofilament, which can have a circular or oval cross-section. The latter section is far more resistant to tangling, which is possibly the only disadvantage of monofilament as a backing material. This particular set-up of shooting head and monofilament backing is ideally suited to such long-distance casting techniques as the 'double haul', enabling experienced practitioners to cast 50 yards or more with ease.

A further benefit is conferred upon the angler hooking a fish at long range, or in very deep water, namely that the fly line is, by its very nature, relatively thick, offering considerable resistance to the water. Thus, there is a risk when using a full line and playing a fish at long range that the pressure exerted by the water against the line can pull the hook clean out or even cause the leader to break. This risk is greatly minimized by the use of a short line and fine backing.

'Torpedo' and 'long belly'

Just as the shooting head is merely a variation upon the forward taper profile, so are there other variations, such as the 'torpedo' taper and the 'long belly', although the principle remains virtually the same in every case. That section of the line which carries the weight necessary to action the rod correctly and enable efficient casting is found towards one end of the line, so that the line is no longer reversible, unlike the double taper.

Manufacturers have developed their own specific descriptions for the line densities now produced, and in order not to confuse the issue for newcomers to fly fishing, it is probably as well to discuss individually the densities in common use, offering brief comments on the function of each.

Floating lines

Floating lines are ideal for the presentation of sunken flies which require little 'working' through the water, or require to be worked very close to the surface, either in stillwater or gently flowing rivers. The depth at which a sunken fly can be fished in stillwater is restricted by the length of the leader—on average some 3-4 yards. It takes quite a long time for an unweighted nymph to sink to that depth, and when trout are feeding close to the bed of a lake, it is common practice to use a dressing containing lead to speed the sink.

On the other hand, where the fish are feeding off the bottom, application of floatant to the leader will ensure that the nymph does not sink too deep. Sometimes, when the fish are feeding and sporting at the surface—and this is particularly common in reservoirs—a lure is fished on a floating line, stripped back so quickly that it skips across the surface, creating a definite wake.

Neutral density lines

Neutral density lines are the modern equivalent of the old silk line, requiring the application of a floatant if they are to be used as a floating line, or used untreated as a slow sinking line. The main advantage of this line was that a suitable length of the tip could be left ungreased, allowing it to sink, and enabling a sunk fly to be fished at greater depth than would be possible with a standard floater. This has now been superseded by the sink tip line.

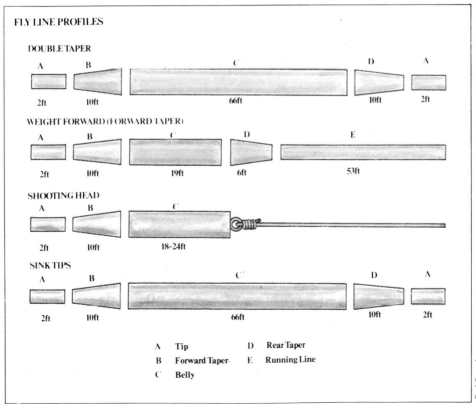

FLY LINE PROFILES

DOUBLE TAPER

A	B	C	D	A
2ft	10ft	66ft	10ft	2ft

WEIGHT FORWARD (FORWARD TAPER)

A	B	C	D	E
2ft	10ft	19ft	6ft	53ft

SHOOTING HEAD

A	B	C
2ft	10ft	18–24ft

SINK TIPS

A	B	C	D	A
2ft	10ft	66ft	10ft	2ft

A Tip   D Rear Taper
B Forward Taper   E Running Line
C Belly

Rod Sutterby

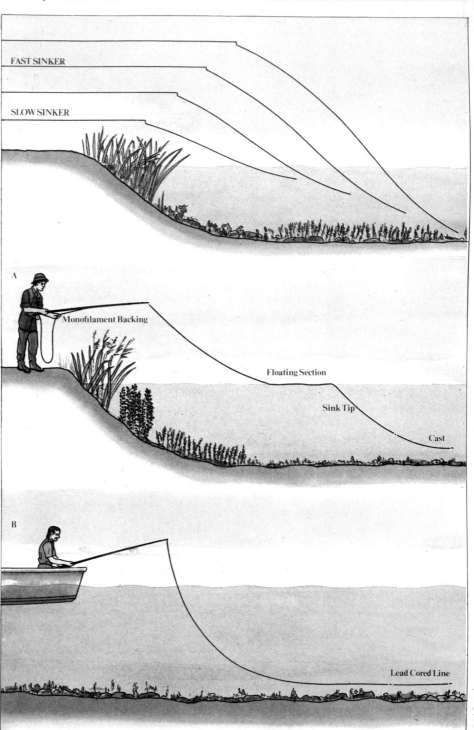

FAST SINKER

SLOW SINKER

A

Monofilament Backing

Floating Section

Sink Tip

Cast

B

Lead Cored Line

Rod Sutterby

Sink tip line

This is carefully manufactured so that the tip, which sinks at medium rate, is adequately supported by the floating body of the line. When fishing a nymph in deepish water, the 'take' is readily signalled by a movement of the floating section. It is equally efficient at indicating a take 'on the drop' (as the fly sinks), and with its use a faster retrieve of the nymph, fly or lure is possible than with the full floating line, because the pattern in use will not rise to the surface as readily as with the floater. This type of line can be very effective in deeper, or medium-flowing rivers, where it is important that depth is achieved quickly and maintained, or in stillwaters where the margins are full of snags which would tend to foul a full sinker. Some anglers claim to find difficulty in casting a sink tip line because of the imbalance between the dense tip and the less dense body, but this can usually be overcome by practice.

Slow sinking lines

With slow sinking lines, the term 'slow' can vary in meaning from manufacturer to manufacturer, because there has never been standardization of terms in this context, but matters seem to be improving, with many firms now offering a full range of densities, so that if a slow sinker is purchased from a range which includes medium and fast sinkers the angler is on safe ground.

The use of a slow sinker does not greatly differ from that of a sink tip, in that it can be used to take fish 'on the drop', or at slow to medium speed retrieve in stillwaters, and in the medium-running or deeper rivers. Nymphs can be fished on slow sinkers, but more commonly the larger wet flies and lures are used. The take of a fish is signalled, as with all sinking lines, by that familiar tug transmitted to the retrieving hand.

Medium sinking lines

Medium sinkers, as may be expected, sink faster than the slow sinkers, and are therefore more suited to deeper or faster-flowing water, and to faster than medium speed retrieves. However, with maximum speed lure stripping, the lure itself will rise very close to the surface, which can be an advantage when the fish are working in the upper levels but demand a fast moving lure which does not break the surface.

Fast sinking lines

Fast sinkers enable fast working of a fly in deep water and ensure that no matter how fast the retrieve, the lure will be unlikely to rise above midwater. Obviously they are well suited to the fast-flowing rivers where the trout or salmon are taking fairly deep.

Very fast sinking lines

Very fast sinkers are fairly specialized lines, often carrying lead in the core. By their nature they are ideal for the very deepest reservoirs, lakes and lochs where the quarry is feeding deep, and where it is important that a lure stripped quickly does not rise much above the bottom. Similarly, they are ideal for the biggest, fastest-flowing rivers, enabling the angler to remain in close touch with his fly throughout every cast. In a big stillwater where the bed snags the fly regularly on slower retrieves, it is a useful dodge to shorten the leader, and attach a dressing incorporating buoyancy material, such as Ethafoam, so that the fly floats up off the bottom clear of the snags, allowing retrieval to be slowed right down.

Lead-cored lines

There is one other type of line coming into use for fishing the deepest reservoirs and lakes—the level lead-cored line, without doubt the fastest sinker of all. This is not used for normal sunken fly fishing, but for trolling behind a boat which may be drifting, or propelled by oars or even a motor, depending upon local rules and regulations.

The purpose of the exercise is to drag the largest size of lure at a steady speed across the bottom, in the hope of attracting those very large trout which have adopted a bottom-feeding existence. It could be argued that this is not true fly fishing, being merely a minor variation on spinning tactics, but the fact is that a form of fly is being used, and so it really is a branch of fly fishing, although unorthodox.

Leaders

A fly is not attached direct to the fly line as the line's bulk would frighten off fish, and so a thinner line, the leader, joins the fly to the reel line. The *leader* is where the action is. The *point*, at the end of the leader, is where the action starts. Too thick a point and fish shy off or take short. Too fine, and the action is dead in seconds when leader and point part company. With a fish on, the leader and point must withstand every surge of its muscle-packed body, fins and tail; every slash of a leaping fish jerking its head to throw the hook. It must survive the hook twisting and wrenching in its nylon-knot socket, stretching and recoiling to absorb shocks before they hit the rod tip, and certainly before the angler reacts.

All this is expected of a piece of nylon some 0.15mm in diameter if you are using a 3lb b.s. point. At 4lb the point is still only 0.18mm, and even a 7lb point has a diameter of only 0.225mm.

Penny a point

A hundred yards of good quality nylon costs about £1. A point costs about a penny, and if you tie your own leaders, they cost between 10p and 15p. What is the purpose of £100-worth of carbon fibre rod and magnesium reel if a pennyworth of nylon fails? There is no sense in using last year's nylon or leftover leaders.

Above all it is important to change a point or leader whenever there is reason to doubt it. If it kinks, twists, necks or gathers a wind knot, take no chances—get rid of it.

Most leaders are between 9 and 15ft long from butt to point. A tapered leader is usually composed of many pieces of nylon, each with a progressively smaller diameter and joined together with knots. One or several droppers (flies set above the terminal or point fly) may be attached to this by more knots. With so many knots, you must be utterly confident of your knotsmanship. Alternatively, you can rely on someone else's

and buy made-up leaders. Most competent fishermen prefer to tie their own.

Use knots in which you have faith. The ordinary dropper knot will not let you down, but it is a bit tricky to tie, especially at the waterside. If you have trouble with it, use the water knot, which is easy to make. Many people tie this latter knot with as many as a dozen turns, but four are adequate.

Knotless tapers

An expensive alternative is to use manufactured knotless tapers, either for the whole leader or just for the tail end. These tapers turn over sweetly, reduce the risk of tangles during casting in gusty weather, and are available in a variety of sizes. Altogether they are excellent—but you cannot buy them for a penny a yard!

ALTERNATIVE TO NEEDLE KNOT

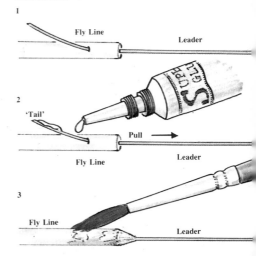

RESERVOIR LEADER FOR SINGLE FLY OR LURE

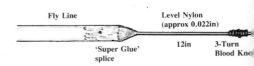

If you make your own leaders, a half-dozen 100-yard spools of different breaking strains are all you need for a season. Breaking strains of 12, 10, 8, 6 and 4lb should be an adequate range. Store the spools in a light-proof box to prevent deterioration and make up a couple of dozen leaders at a sitting. These can then be stored in marked envelopes in your tackle bag for selection at the waterside.

Spare line for points

Points have to be renewed occasionally on the bank, however. Carry a 50-yard spool of 3–7lb b.s. line (whatever you use) in your tackle bag for this purpose.

Opinions differ widely both about whether a leader should be tapered or not, and, if tapered, on how to taper it. Many successful reservoir anglers regularly fish simple 10–14ft level (untapered) lengths of 6lb or 7lb nylon. Others go to great trouble to taper their casts with six or seven lengths of nylon

(Left) How to make a Super Glue splice.
(Below) The efficient plastic cast connector.
(At foot) Dimensions of a reservoir leader.

1. Having perforated fly line (left) thread leader butt through.

2. Apply small amount of 'Super Glue 3' to tail. Without delay pull cast so as to draw 'tail' back into fly line.
   Roll between two flat surfaces to straighten join.

3. Apply 2-3 coats of liquid PVC to finish.

USING A CAST CONNECTOR

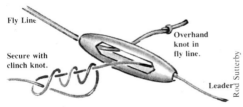

Fly Line

Secure with
clinch knot.

Overhand
knot in
fly line.

Leader

Rod Sutterby

of differing diameters. In the early days of reservoir trouting, a double-tapered (tapered at both ends) leader, with a heavy belly to assist turnover, was very popular. This had as many as a dozen knots in it, but in the right hands it was very successful. Nevertheless, these complex tapers are now rare, although some anglers do use a simpler form of double taper.

The level leader is quite suitable for fishing heavy flies and lures, but less effective for lighter flies and small nymphs. Generally, the leader should be tapered to suit the point size. On many small streams, a 4lb point would be rather coarse, but few anglers go below 3lb except on special occasions. On most reservoirs you can expect to hook fish up to 3lb, or even 6–8lb if you are fortunate. In such circumstances, a point of 6–8lb b.s. is not too heavy.

Importance of fly size

The size of the fly is also important. A small nymph or fly never sits well on a heavy point and often the size of the hook eye precludes the use of large diameter nylon anyway. For small flies, a 3–5lb point is suitable, according to conditions. Conversely, a large fly or a heavy lure, especially a two or three-hook lure, sits awkwardly on too fine a point. A heavy lure imposes severe strains on light points during casting, and it is also prone to flick back and tangle with the point. In such cases, 6–8lb b.s. should be considered, especially if big fish are expected.

Sometimes your fishing style or local water conditions demand the use of a long leader, even though these are difficult to handle in boisterous weather. A long leader fished deep is often very effective. Much depends on how well you cast, and it is worth

Vary length of this section according to total leader length required.	3-Turn Blood Knot	Knotless Taper 0.020-0.011in (approx)	If finer point preferred add 18in 0.009in nylon.
0-72in		72in	

Leaders

G. L. Carlisle

A good leader proves itself by the way the fly line acts in the forward cast. With a long leader your fly casting must be good.

practising to get the rhythm right. In stormy weather or high wind, when the surface is rough and the fish are taking on top, you may require a *shorter* 'storm' leader.

Many anglers like to tie an 18in nylon 'leg' directly to the reel line and attach their leaders to this. It gets shortened inch by inch as the season wears on, and you may have to renew it at intervals. Attach it to the reel line with a needle knot or a nylon whipping. Whip over the knot and varnish it so that it slides easily through the top rings of the rod. Nothing is worse than having it stick in the tip ring when you are about to net a fish.

Check the connector knots

If you do not feel competent about attaching a leg smoothly, use plastic leader connectors. These sometimes have a rough finish, so rub them over with fine sand paper before use. It is also worth colouring them to suit your line. A green or brown felt-tip pen does the job admirably. Make sure the connector knots, both in the reel line and the nylon leg, are well made and do not slip through the connector under strain.

Some anglers advocate a loop at the end of the leg, with a similar loop to attach the leader. Two loops, however, often cause an undesirable 'wake' in the water, as well as being prone to catch up with the hook in flight during casting. The author prefers a water knot for leader attachment, although it means the legs need replacing frequently.

When not to use a dropper

Many anglers who consistently take good fish never use a dropper. Others regularly fish one or even two or three. When shortlining from bank or boat, a team of three flies can be very useful to indicate the taking fly, and sometimes the taking depth. But with long casting, things are different. Even a single dropper can drive you to distraction on a blustery day, although if you can manage it the fish often take the dropper rather than the tail fly. Perhaps it is the fly, perhaps the way it fishes on the dropper, perhaps it is the depth.

Many anglers forego the dropper after dusk, chiefly because of the hazard of fouling, but if you are shortlining with a team of buzzers, with care they are perfectly manageable even then. You can always easily cut them off.

Spacing the droppers

On professionally manufactured casts, the common practice is to fix droppers at 3ft intervals, which is fine if you fish that way. Many anglers using only one dropper, however, prefer it to be set halfway along the cast. This makes it more effective as a bobber during the last stages of the retrieve, and prevents the tail fly coming up too far at the same time. The length of the leader is probably the most important factor in deciding on how many and where to place droppers.

Colour is considered important by some. Nylon can be bought in various shades, or you can dye it instead. If a leader is coiled first, you can immerse half in dye, dry it out, and then immerse the other half in a different colour. This produces a splendid camouflage, and if it gives you confidence it is worth trying.

There are no rules when it comes to leaders. Experiment with likely patterns; then make up your own to suit your style.

Arthur Ogelsley

Dry flies

Dry fly fishing has always been regarded as the supreme art in fly fishing circles. This is particularly so on rivers and chalk-streams where matching the hatch is only the beginning of the problem and where presentation has to be considered as well. But dry flies also play an important part in reservoir and lake fishing where trout are attracted by insects on the surface.

Favourite season

Of all the periods during the season when trout rise to a dry fly, the favourite is the time that the mayfly hatch. The huge flies emerge from the water in such large numbers that the trout literally gorge themselves to capacity, and the better fish rise freely. On these occasions almost any artificial pattern representing a mayfly will take fish. Unfortunately the mayfly only hatches in running water and in a few privileged lakes, so does not affect fishing everywhere.

Early in the season the hawthorn fly hatches in large numbers and very good catches can be made with the aid of a Black Gnat. Again this mostly applies to running waters, but vast numbers of hawthorn flies were noticed at Rutland Water. Although the fish were not rising to them at that time,

they will most probably do so in the future.

In late summer, one of the most popular flies that hatches on every water is the sedge. These medium-sized flies start to hatch in July and August and are present throughout the day, and in vast numbers at nightfall. If weather conditions are good and flies are hatching, a pattern representing a sedge can be very effective, for the 'spent' sedge falling back upon the water is the fly most likely to attract the attention of the trout. But they are by no means the only ones. Throughout the year there are hatches of buzzers, the dreaded caenis, which is too small to be imitated, and a number of Ephemerids such as the olives.

Land-borne insects

These insects all hatch from the water and return there to lay their eggs, and this is when the trout rise to them. In addition to these insects, there are also the land-borne kind which live and breed on dry land but are often carried onto the water by winds. Naturally these flies are more important to the reservoir angler because the large expanses of water are too much for the insects to fly across while maintaining a battle with the wind to stay in the air. They

G. L. Carlisle

(Left) These mayfly duns, newly hatched, will rest until they become spinners which swarm near the water to mate. Afterwards the females will return to the water to deposit their eggs. During a hatch the mayfly will cluster thickly on waterside vegetation even on anglers' clothing.

(Above) Silicone mucilage is applied to an artificial mayfly to ensure that it floats temptingly on the surface of the water.

(Right) After the flotant has been applied—as in the photograph above—the artificial mayfly sits on the surface film in imitation of the natural insect.

P. H. Ward/Natural Science Photos

71

then make a meal for any lurking trout.

Of the insects that hatch on land, the daddy long legs is the one which, year after year, adds to the larder of the trout.

In the late summer the daddies hatch in vast number in the bankside vegetation, and being fairly weak fliers, are easily carried onto the water when the wind rises. The trout then cruise the margins and wind lanes taking the daddy long legs with a great swirl or splash, and fantastic sport can be had with a natural or imitation fly.

Difficult match

The drone-fly also features on the trout's menu for a short period when it is present in sufficient numbers, and also another land-borne insect, the ladybird. Both of these are rather difficult to match, and it is often a question of sorting through the box; but once a pattern is found, sport becomes brisk.

The other land insect that really interests the trout is the flying ant. On rare occasions a swarm of these insects is blown onto the water and the trout feed heavily on them, so it is wise to have an imitation in the box, just in case. The same also applies to bees and grasshoppers, but there are few recorded patterns of these insects. When trout are seen taking them the angler must be ready to tie an acceptable imitation.

Patterns of dry fly

In almost all instances where trout feed on land-borne insects, the rule is not to move the fly. It is not possible to simulate the vibrating motion of their legs and in any case they are soon dead or exhausted and then lay still. An imitation is far more likely to succeed if it is cast out and then left. Regarding the patterns of dry fly that are needed, every angler should include in his collection the following: Tupp's Indispensible, Mayfly, Sedge, Black Gnat, Grey Duster, Iron Blue, Daddy Long Legs, Sherry Spinner, Pond Olive, Lunn's Particular, Flying Ant and Drone Fly. These are by no means all the patterns available, but equipped with them in varying sizes the angler should be able to deal with almost every circumstance he is likely to meet in rivers, lakes and streams.

Bill Howes

(Left) Harvey Torbett carefully selecting a suitable artificial fly while trout fishing on a West Country reservoir.
(Top, right) Some dry fly artificials which can be matched to the natural insect: 1 Iron Blue Dun; 2 Black Gnat; 3 Olive Dun; 4 Daddy Long Legs; 5 Brown Sedge; 6 Grey Duster.
(Right) In the chart, the black lines show times of the year when certain kinds of insect may be expected to be found. The angler is advised to have the tied artificials with him at these periods. From 1 to 6, the natural fly is in bold type; the artificial is in italics.

Tourist Photo Library

MATCHING THE HATCH

Natural *Artificial*	May	June	July	August	September	October	
1 Caenis *Grey Duster*			————————			1	
2 Daddy Long Legs *Daddy Long Legs*					————	2	
3 Flying Ant – during heat waves *Black Ant*			———————		3		
4 Hawthorn Fly *Hawthorn Fly*	————				4		
5 Mayfly *Mayfly*	2nd week ———— 2nd week			5			
6 Sedge Fly *Wickhams Fancy*		last 2 weeks ———— first 2 weeks		6			

Lyn Cawley

73

Wet flies

In contrast to the dry fly, intended to imitate or simulate an insect floating or alighting on the water's surface, the wet fly is used to imitate a small insect or creature living and actively moving *below* the surface.

This fundamental difference of function is reflected in the manner of tying the fly and in the materials used. Although some fly patterns can be tied either for dry or wet fly fishing, each is distinctive to its purpose. Stiff cock hackles are necessary for a floating fly, but softer, easily wetted hackles help the wet fly to sink, as well as providing a semblance of limb movement when the fly is working by the action of the stream, or during retrieval.

Wet flies may be winged or wingless, fully hackled or with 'spider' type hackles, or even with reduced and lighter 'throat' hackles, according to type. In some cases there are permutations of these variables.

Winged wet flies

The winged wet flies are probably the best known, and several important wet flies such as the Mallard and Claret and the Teal and Red may be tied in numerous variations of colour, providing a whole series of alternatives on the main theme. Good examples are Mallard and Claret, Mallard and Black, and Mallard and Mixed. Other popular winged flies are the Golden Olive, March Brown, and the Connemara Black. These are usually tied with reduced or thin hackles at the throat.

Palmer tied flies

Other winged flies are built up with full hackles wound along the whole length of the hook shank, and even with small additional 'throat' hackles as well. These are exemplified by the famous Invicta and Wickham's Fancy. Sometimes the hackle is replaced with teased-out hair or wool, as in the case of the Gold Ribbed Hare's Ear.

Flies tied with the hackle extending along the length of the body are said to be Palmer tied, after the Palmer, which may be black,

(Right) Nymphs, left to right: Orange Buzzer, Tiger Nymph, Coryxa, Pheasant Tail, Shrimp, Partridge and Orange, Amber Nymph.
(Below) Wet flies, left to right: Invicta, Greenwell's Glory, Mallard and Claret, Royal Coachman, Woodcock and Green, Black and Peacock Spider.

red, or ginger. This is the prototype wet fly, tied wingless but with a full body hackle. A further excellent and killing example of this type is the Zulu.

Spider hackled flies

A further group of important wingless flies is typified by the Black Pennel. This is made up with a slim body, a short tail whisk, and a full shoulder hackle tied in at the head only. Another example is the Black and Peacock Spider, an excellent fly when fish are feeding on snail. The Snipe and Purple, and the Partridge and Orange are also of this type.

Nymphs

Nymphs are quite different in make-up, appearance and function. They are intended to imitate or simulate the larval forms of many underwater insects. The best known are probably the Pheasant Tail and the buzzer series of nymphs. There are also green nymphs, brown nymphs and black nymphs, all excellent in the right place at the right time.

Nymphs are often tied with an imitation thorax and wing cases, as well as a banded or

ringed appearance to represent the segmented abdomen common in many natural nymph forms. These may also have tiny hackles or hairs built in to give that important suggestion of moving limbs. Others may represent small adult beetles common in many waters. The Corixa, tied with imitation hard wing cases, is a good example.

Within each of the groups broadly described there are some examples intended to be accurate imitations of the natural insect, and others are intended to caricature or simulate a whole group of similar looking creatures. Examples of winged artificial flies are the Invicta and the Greenwell's Glory.

Important artificials

Other important artificial flies are the distinctive flies made up with gold or silver tinsel or with brilliant fluorescent colours, which owe their success to their capacity for triggering off the predatory instincts of fish in much the same way that is achieved by a small spinner.

The Jersey Herd is a nymph of this kind, and is very effective when fished fairly fast in deep water. The Bloody Butcher, Alexandra, and Dunkeld are examples of winged attractors. There are also many small fish imitations such as the Polystickle, which introduces one final grouping generally known as Lures, most of which are intended to imitate small fish.

Lures

Lures are usually tied on long-shanked hooks, or on two or three small hooks tied in twos. They can be between 1in and 3in in length, with flashy or coloured bodies and large wings over the shank, made of whole

Black Lure and Muddler Minnow. The Red Terror is an exotic salmon lure.

Wet fly action

Whatever the type, the wet fly often depends far more on its action in the water when fished, than upon its resemblance to a particular insect. When trout are feeding freely the actual pattern is not important, but when the fish are preoccupied or need tempting the angler must use his ingenuity to discover what the fish are feeding upon, and imitate it as best he can. Often, his speed and depth of fishing are also very important.

Unlike his dry fly counterpart, the wet fly angler may fish two or three flies on the same cast, the extra flies being attached to droppers off the cast at intervals of 4 or 5ft. The patterns are selected so that the tail fly can be fished deep, with the bottom dropper in midwater, and the top dropper near to the surface. He can even arrange for his top dropper (fly on a short cast) to dibble above the surface, while fishing the other flies below it. These tactics have the advantage of providing several opportunities to discover the appropriate or 'taking' fly and the required depth. A disadvantage is that a bad back-cast with a team of flies often produces a tangle which takes a long time to clear.

Of all kinds of wet fly, the lures are mostly intended to represent small fish. One of the most well known, the famous Polystickle, might be thought to imitate the stickleback. Some lures are tied on two or three hooks. From left to right: Baby Doll, Missionary, Church Fry, Black Chenille, Whisky Fry, Appetizer, and the Muddler Minnow.

Tourist Photo Library

Salmon flies

Bill Howes

A salmon angler with a fine range of flies kept in an orderly state. Few working fly boxes look like this!

Evolving from the early trout flies, the contemporary salmon fly shows little evidence to associate it with the imitation of natural insects. It is generally considered that early salmon flies were tied in ignorance of what the salmon actually thought they were, and only recently has it been realized that salmon do not feed while travelling to their spawning grounds in freshwater.

Shape, style and character

Colour has always been considered important of course, but as the ideas of one fly dresser are not necessarily those of his contemporaries, almost every known combination became available. In spite of this variety of colour, a great similarity among the patterns as to shape, style and character emerged. Type, size and presentation were considered less important than they are today: the reason being, perhaps, the greater abundance of salmon earlier this century.

The gaudy fly is still produced for fishing, but more as a fly-tying exercise than anything else. The more durable and easily produced hair-winged fly is brightly coloured, however, because it provides a better imitation of a natural insect. Indeed, the gaudy fly will always win over a drab one.

Such names as 'Jock Scott', 'Black Doctor', 'Blue Doctor', 'Blue Charm', 'Chalmers', 'Dunkeld', 'Thunder and Lightning', 'Durham Ranger' and 'Dusty Miller', 'Green Highlander' and 'Green King', the 'Logie', and many others, have become well-known to salmon fishermen.

Art form

An object as colourful as the traditional salmon fly lends itself as an art form, and probably for this reason alone its survival is assured, even though it has lost much of its practical popularity on the angling scene.

Modern flies with hair wings still retain the original brightness of the traditional ones, particularly regarding bodies, tails and hackles. In most instances these are retained in their entirety, only the wings being different. The hairs used for these wings are usually dyed the same bright shades of red,

Irish Tourist Board

The materials from which salmon flies are tied are very colourful. A gaudy fly will catch fish when drab ones fail.

Hardy's

A range of moose-hair salmon flies. The large flies at the foot are a 'Dusty Miller' and a 'Green Highlander', with a 'Hairy Mary' and a 'Thunder and Lightning' above. Small salmon flies should be fished between 3 and 5in below the surface.

blue, yellow, green and orange, but in some instances they are left in their natural state. The 'Blue Charm' is a good illustration of this, as the teal and mallard flank feathers of the original patterns are replaced by either brown bucktail fibres or brown squirrel tail fibres, according to the size of hook. To distinguish between the two dressings, the hair-winged version of the 'Blue Charm' was called 'Hairy Mary'.

Size of fly

Having decided on the kind of fly, you then have to choose how it shall be fished. The size of a salmon fly is most important; colour only secondary. The size used will depend largely on the height, temperature and colour of the water, and on weather conditions. If a salmon follows your fly or rises short this usually means that the fly is too big or your leader is too thick. The best way to start is to use a small fly—you can always increase the size later. As a general rule: the bigger the river, the larger the fly. A larger fly would also be used in coloured water, in very rough or broken water, or in deep holes that have a dark bottom. In conditions where wind, light and temperature are constant, a medium-sized fly is recommended. Low, clear water, usually referred to as 'summer' conditions, favours a much smaller fly, and usually one of a more sombre hue. One would also use this kind over a light-coloured shallow bottom. Another rule therefore is always to try to use a fly in colour contrast to its surroundings.

General and specific patterns

Flies tied on what are called 'Ordinary' or 'Rational' hooks are referred to as 'Standard' patterns, whereas those used for summer conditions are called 'Low Water' patterns. These latter patterns are often merely scaled down versions of Standard patterns, tied on hooks of a lighter gauge wire, and the dressings taken well forward of the hook bend.

Salmon flies

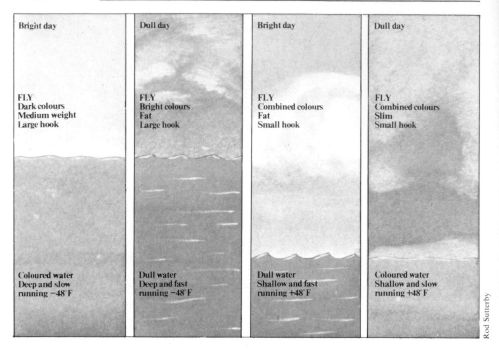

Bright day	Dull day	Bright day	Dull day
FLY Dark colours Medium weight Large hook	FLY Bright colours Fat Large hook	FLY Combined colours Fat Small hook	FLY Combined colours Slim Small hook
Coloured water Deep and slow running −48°F	Dull water Deep and fast running −48°F	Dull water Shallow and fast running +48°F	Coloured water Shallow and slow running +48°F

Rod Sutterby

The chart provides some general hints on the selection of large and small salmon flies according to the types of water and existing weather conditions.

In addition to these general patterns there are others which are designed for specific rivers. Two of the best known are the 'Spey' and the 'Dee' patterns (named after the rivers), made with rather sombre materials.

These flies are used in the early part of the season when the temperature can be at almost freezing point. They are dressed lightly on very large hooks, 3in being quite common, and this combination of lightness of dressing and heaviness of hook means that the flies sink deeper. They are therefore more likely to come within the field of view of the fish which lies close to the bottom when the temperature of the water is very low. In addition to the suitability of these large flies for the particular circumstances in which they are used, one of their best features is the extreme mobility of their hackles and wings, giving them a very lifelike appearance when they are worked in the water. In contrast to the gaudy flies described earlier, 'Spey' and 'Dee' flies are a very practical kind of pattern.

Satisfactory alternative

'Prawn' or 'Shrimp' fly as the name implies, is a fly version of the crustacean which forms part of the staple diet of the growing salmon during its life in the sea. These can be very successful during the early part of the season, and one theory is that they are attacked by the fish through force of habit rather than from a desire to feed. They also make a satisfactory alternative for dedicated fly fishermen who do not wish to 'spin the natural prawn'—a very popular method of salmon fishing on some waters.

The fly specifically produced for Irish waters is usually more heavily dressed than standard patterns, and is designed with harmonious body colour schemes. Its impression of warmth and rich colour is ideally suited to the peaty waters of Ireland.

Fly dressing is a very advanced craft and there are many books of instruction available. Your local tackle dealer should be able to tell you which are the most informative.

Fly tying

Anglers have used artificial as well as natural flies for centuries. Perhaps the idea of making artificial lures occurred when supplies of natural flies dried up and the angler decided to attempt a copy by binding fur and hair to a hook. The pattern of fly used depends on the conditions prevailing in the fishing water and on the kind of flies which occur naturally.

The basic fly

To create even a rough impression of a fly some knowledge of its anatomy is needed. The head, which is not simulated on many tied flies, is set on a body which is divided into two sections—the upper, larger thorax and the abdomen. The wings vary in size but can be represented by different hackles, usually made from pieces of feather.

Because dry flies, as their name suggests, are intended to float on the surface, lightness and buoyancy in their construction are most important. The tying must be tight and even to prevent waterlogging. Where heavy or porous materials would add to the attractiveness, these are given a last-minute coating of a suitable oil to help keep the fly afloat.

For tying your own flies a small fly-tying vice is essential. Select a model that has a firm base, covers most of the hook by gripping the sharp end, and can be tilted upwards to allow ample access to the fly. Hackle pliers are needed to hold the hackle firm and to prevent it from unwinding when released. Scissors with short, pointed blades are required for trimming. A scalpel can be used instead, but great care must be taken as this instrument can cause nasty wounds. A cake of cobbler's wax will also be needed before you can begin to produce your own artificial flies. A good selection of materials, including pieces of fur, tinsel, hair, feathers on the skin, wool, and silk thread, should be to hand as, after basic methods have been mastered, experimental and unusual varieties can be created.

(*Above*) *Donald Downes, well-known fly tier.* (*Overleaf*) *Fly tying equipment including vice hackles, hackle pliers, silks, scissors, feathers and whip finishing tool.*

There are other useful, though not essential, accessories. Among these are tweezers, bobbin-holders, and a whip-finish tool which completes the tying with a neat knot. The angler is now ready to tie a basic fly along the following lines.

A trout hook (size 14-11) is held in the vice with the shank and eye protruding horizontally and the barb clamped out of sight. The basic body is constructed out of about 10in of tying silk or a silk floss (which is fluffy and covers more easily). To make this first layer adhere, either coat the shank with vinyl glue or run the silk through fingertips that have been rubbed with cobbler's wax. Beginning 3-4in behind the eye, wind the silk neatly

Riallo-Bast

Bill Howes

along the shank, binding down the loose end with the first few turns and finish where the bend of the hook begins. If using tying silk, about 100 turns to the inch will be necessary, while the silk floss will cover the same length in far fewer turns. At this stage the tail is added, and for this the end of the thread is left hanging down, gripped by the pliers.

A tail can be made from the hairs of such animals as the badger and squirrel, or from the fronds of a stiff feather. These should be bunched and tied securely—so that the fly does not gradually moult—before being positioned at the bend of the hook and bound to the shank with the remaining tying silk or floss. A few passes under the bunched hairs as well as over them will cock the tail up jauntily.

Binding in the tail

When securing the tail, bind in the material for the body. A stripped poultry quill, softened in water, is good for building on top of the silk because its overlapping turns round the shaft will resemble abdominal segments. Wind on the quill towards the eye and fasten it down with tying silk. Tinsel or steel wool strands to add glitter can be bound in during the body's construction, and a thorax furnished out of materials with interesting textures, such as chenille or angora wool.

The bodies of the less streamlined flies are dressed or 'dubbed' with animal fur—mole skin for example—which is bound to the hook shaft with silk or wire. A foundation of cobbler's wax is needed, and the modern substitute, 'Vycoat', makes it possible to 'sculpt' a shapely foundation before dubbing on fur for a plump, succulent appearance. 'Vycoat' can be moulded into a glossy black head, which cleverly conceals any loose ends. Generally, the loose ends of thread left after every process can be held in and concealed by the next stage. The final thread, unless a moulded head is constructed, should be secured with a neat whip finish near the eye.

Hackles are feathers from the collar plumage of birds, and hackling is the reproduction of bristles at the shoulder of an

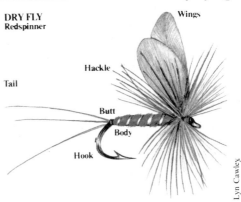

DRY FLY
Redspinner

Wings

Hackle

Tail

Butt

Body

Hook

Lyn Cawley

artificial fly. In dry fly tying the feathers of aquatic birds are best for buoyancy, although poultry cock hackles are equally good as they are stiff, glossy and water repellent. Natural colours are varied, but dyeing can make the variety infinite.

To prepare a feather for hackling hold it by the tip and run moistened fingers down the fibres so that they stand out at right angles and separate. Then, having stripped the base of the quill, lay the feather at right angles to the hook-eye and lash the bared quill to the shank with tying silk. The fronded remainder is then held at the tip with hackle pliers and three or four turns made towards the tail. The weight of the pliers hanging down from the tip will prevent your work from springing undone while freeing your hands to fasten it with a couple of turns of silk. Next, cut off the tip of the feather. One basic hackle fly, the 'Palmer', is hackled along the whole length of its body, so more than one feather is needed.

Binding the hackle

Binding a hackle needs a steady hand since the binding (gilt wire in a 'Palmer') is pulled between each separate fibre of the feather: to keep these fibres from being crushed the wire needs to be kept taut throughout and drawn clockwise, then anti-clockwise, and so on, alternating between each fibre. The finished hackle should be fluffed out with a sharp needle. Wire binding in the 'Palmer' makes not only for durability but also for an attractive effect.

Fly tying

TYING A DRY FLY

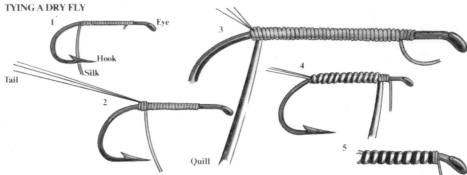

TYING IN THE HACKLE

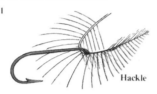

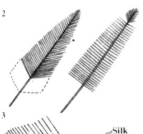

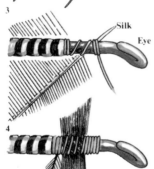

TYING IN THE WINGS

Tying a dry fly *(above)*. Begin by winding the silk to the position *(1)*; the quill is tied-in at the tail *(2)* then the silk wound back to the front after the tail of stiff hackle fibres is attached. Give the tail an upwards tilt by running one turn under it. The ribbed body is formed by winding a stripped quill down to the and tie-off using the silk. Tying-in the hackle *(left)*. Select a hackle whose fibres match the distance between the point and the eye *(1)*. Trim the hackle as in *(2)* and pass it through the fingers to make the fibres stand out. The bared stem can now be tied on *(3)*. A few turns of the hackle from the eye leave you at position *(4)*. Bed it down with the silk still hanging down on hackle pliers and tie-off finally with a whip-finish. Tying-in the wings *(right)*. These must be matched pairs *(1)* either side of a feather. Hold them securely, following the turns in Nos. 2 to 6.

Rod Sutterby

ARTIFICIAL BAIT

DRY FLY

NYMPH

WET FLY

LURE

NATURAL FOOD

MAYFLY NYMPH

THREE SPINED
STICKLEBACK
(Breeding Colours)

CATERPILLAR
(Chalk Blue)

SUMMER MAYFLY

Lyn Cawley

The simplest of dry flies—the 'Snipe' and 'Black Spider'—are simply hook, hackle and silk, but with natural colours or by dyeing this combination affords many possibilities. The addition of wings, however, can improve the balance of a dry (floating) fly and of course makes for more spectacular creations. They can be tied in at the same stage as the tail and the fastening shanks concealed when the body is built up. Alternatively, a space can be left between thorax and hook-eye, and the wings added when the body is complete, although there needs to be some silk round the shank before wings can be attached successfully.

Double wings

Dry flies often sport double wings which also makes them more buoyant. Two feathers are needed from symmetrically identical positions on either side of a bird's wing or tail fan. Symmetrically matched sections are cut from the centre of these feathers. These diamond-shaped sections have to be torn in half (for the double-wing effect) and eased into rectangles between finger and thumb (without the fibres separating). The 'wings' are rounded off with scissors and the four butt ends pinched firmly between finger and thumb and introduced at the shoulder, two on either side of the body.

Only practice, patience and steady hands

Many artificial flies are tied to match the natural counterpart. The wet lure apes the caterpillar or grub, the dry fly has all the appearance of a Mayfly. Nymphs resemble the real insect larva on weed-stems, while the polystickle imitates a stickleback.

make for successful wing tying. A loop of silk has to be squeezed between finger and feather, over the body, and down between feather and thumb. It requires concentration, but three turns of silk must be firmly drawn down without the wings splitting. To finish off, wind the thread in front of and behind the wings, passing it between them to keep them separate. The knots will be concealed by any hackle added afterwards—and often winged flies run to two hackles behind the wings and another pair in front. What perplexes the beginner is finding the space along a normal hook shaft for all these ornamentations.

Flies for coarse fish

The varieties of dry fly patterns have occupied many volumes, and the possibilities are not yet exhausted. Moreover, their use is no longer, as was traditionally the case, restricted to fishing for trout and salmon, for such coarse fish as rudd, roach, chub, dace, grayling, perch and pike are all taken on artificial flies.

New trout patterns

The last ten years has been unique in the history of fly-tying for two reasons. First, more new trout fly patterns have been produced than possibly during any other period of the same length. Second, from this explosion of new patterns there has emerged an unusually large number of dressings that dramatically break with tradition. Their impact has been immediate. Almost overnight the art of fly-tying in this country was turned on its head.

Revolutionary methods

These new patterns introduced revolutionary methods of dressing a fly and precipitated experimentation with new materials. This in turn lead to a re-examination of what it was that induced a trout to take a fly, with the suggestion that a close representation of a natural fly was not necessary. Trout, it is claimed, will take any brightly coloured attractive fly. Such a change was no accident, for it directly coincided with a meteoric rise in the popularity of trout fishing that accompanied the stocking of large public reservoirs and disused lakes and ponds with trout in the mid-Sixties.

With more anglers able to afford quality trout fishing, more time and effort began to be devoted to finding more effective ways of catching them. This meant developing new techniques and, more importantly, new flies to meet the demands of specific problems. Because of this, artificial flies became less a subject of interest to the angler with nothing better to do on the long winter nights of the close season, but the result of thoughtful, practical design. In this search for new ideas, British fly fishermen were quite willing to look to fly fishermen in other countries—France, Sweden, but most notably America—and exchange views. It was in America that the best known, most successful and probably the most innovative of the

TYING MUDDLER SHOULDER

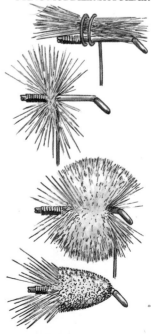

Di Lewis

Rod Sutterby

new patterns of this period had its origins—the Muddler Minnow.

Many people believe that the Muddler Minnow got its name because of the way it moved in the water. They say it confuses the trout into taking it. This is not true. The Muddler Minnow was a direct attempt by its creator, Don Gapen, to tie an exact imitation of the flatheaded Cockotush minnow found in the Nipigon River in northern Ontario, nicknamed 'muddlers' by the locals.

Muddler Minnow

Whereas the majority of flies before the Muddler relied on feather fibres in their construction, the Muddler Minnow is largely made of hair fibres. The part that makes most people tying the Muddler for the first time wish they had never started is the head and shoulders made of deer hair. This material is believed to have been used by North American Indians to make trout lures. However, the method used to tie the head is quite original and certainly not as difficult a task as is often made out.

The space at the head of the hook where the deer hair is to be tied should be left bare.

Muddler Minnow

Hook: 6-12 D/E long shanked hook.
Tying silk: Black.
Tail: A section of oak turkey wing quill that slightly extends the length of the hook.
Body: Flat gold tinsel.
Wing: A bunch of grey squirrel tail hair sandwiched between two sections of oak turkey wing feather. This extends the end of the tail and is tied pointing slightly upwards from the hook.
Shoulders: Deer hair—tied as explained in detail in text.

Chomper

Hook: 10-14 D/E.
Tying silk: Black.
Body: Ostrich herl.
Overbody: Raffine. A strip of polythene is tied behind the hook eye and wound backwards and forwards over hook shank to build up a body.
Head: Tying silk built up to form bold head.

A small bunch of stiff fibres is cut from a deer skin and held horizontally over the hook where the silk has been wound off, having tied in the body and wing. Two loose turns of silk are wound round the fibres and hook shank with enough tension to hold the fibres on the hook so that they need no longer be held in position with your fingers. The silk is then pulled tight and the fur spins like a hackle round the hook shank.

Having done this, the silk should be behind the fibres. Wind the silk through the fibres and make a half-hitch knot. This knot is then pressed close up to the fibres. This operation is repeated 4-5 times depending on the size of the head. Press each 'spinning' close up to the last one until the hook shank has been sufficiently covered. When this is completed, the head of the Muddler should look something like an electrocuted sheepdog. Clip the fibres so that the head is bullet-shaped, leaving some fibres nearest the body to act as a hair hackle.

The Muddler Minnow has been used as the basis for several variations and tied in many different colours using dyed buckskin

Di Lewis

fibres and impala hair, instead of grey squirrel, in the wing. Further additions to the fly have appeared recently in a search for an even more life-like resemblance. A pattern has been developed, for example, with pectoral fins made of pheasant tail fibres.

The Chomper family

The Chomper Family of flies were developed for quite different purposes from the Muddler Minnow. Their creator, the British angler Richard Walker, set out to develop a fly that was simple in design but did not necessarily imitate any one food in particular, but could resemble trout food in general. This idea has earned Chompers the title of 'Impressionistic Flies' rather than precise imitations. They are possibly the easiest of all flies to tie. Simply wind ostrich herl on to the hook shank until it is covered. When a body is formed, lay a back—or shell—of damp raffine over the herl.

Using various different combinations of colours, a variety of trout foods can be loosely imitated using the same tying method. For example, white ostrich herl with a brown or green back looks like Corixa. ostrich herl dyed amber or green with a light brown back looks like a sedge pupa or a shrimp. Because of its simple design, the Chomper can be weighted with thin strips of wine bottle lead under the dressing to make it sink faster without the shape of the fly being dramatically affected. Its adaptability also enables it to be fished in the water at any possible speed.

The Polystickle

Richard Walker is also the originator of the range of flies known as Polystickles, an ingenious imation of sticklebacks, roach and perch fry that trout often feed on in the shallows of the larger lakes. The effectiveness of the Polystickle is without a doubt achieved by the translucent effect of polythene covering the body of the fly. Its success can also be accounted for by its imitating the red and silver 'guts' of the natural by the use of silver hooks and the addition of a layer of crimson floss two-thirds of the way up the hook shank towards the eye that shines through the clear PVC

Di Lewis

used to build up the shape of the body.

The Polystickle's design enables it to sink quickly to the depth of the trout, and being made of almost totally trout-tooth-proof materials has proved itself to be extremely durable. Lastly, the Polystickle can very easily be adapted to deep water and muddy conditions, or when the light is dull—trout moving into the shallow to feed on fry at dusk. To cope with these conditions, a body of white raffine—instead of clear raffine—can be used. Alternatively, white day-light fluorescent wool covered with polythene can be used with a back of orange raffine.

The Grey Wulff

Because the recent interest in trout fishing has been largely centred on stillwaters, it is there that we find the majority of new patterns. However, one fly-tying innovation designed more specifically for river and stream fishing should be mentioned here—the Grey Wulff.

This is a dry fly pattern developed by Lee Wulff of America. The peculiarity of this fly is the way the wings are positioned—sloping forwards over the head of the fly. Instead of feather quill, the wings are tied with a bunch of deer or other hair fibres. This makes the fly a remarkable floater—something few dry flies can claim to be. When tied in various colours and sizes, the Grey Wulff successfully imitates every species of up-winged fly likely to be found on rivers and lakes.

The Grey Wulff has also proven itself a remarkable imitation of the up-winged fly emerging from its nymphal, or larval, form if fished in the surface film instead of dry on top of the surface.

The four patterns discussed here have all displayed their value to thousands of fly fishermen all over the country. They have earned their spurs in terms of number of trout caught and for that reason have also earned a position in the fly-boxes of every fly fisherman. Not many new patterns win this kind of respect.

When considering buying or tying up a new pattern for the first time, remember that innovation alone will not improve your catches.

Polystickle
Hook: 6-12 D/E long shanked hook.
Tying silk: Black.
Tail and back: A strip of dampened raffine.
Body: Open spirals of black tying silk wound two-thirds of the way up the hook.
Throat: Crimson floss silk.
Overbody: A strip of polythene is tied behind the hook eye and wound backwards and forwards over hook shank to build up a body.
Throat hackle: Red or orange hackle fibres tied under hook shank.
Head: Tying silk built up to form bold head.

Grey Wulff
Hook: 10-16 D/E.
Tying silk: Black or olive.
Whisks: Blue dun hackle fibres, or brown barred squirrel fibres.
Body: Grey squirrel fur.
Hackle: Medium blue dun cock hackle.
Wing: Deer hair or small brown barred squirrel hair.

Dr Lewis

Tube flies

Although the tube fly is not a modern innovation, its worldwide popularity is only recent. And although it will probably never oust the standard and low-water flies tied on a normal single and double hooks, there is no doubt that it is here to stay. The tube fly, as its name denotes, consists of a length of polythene or metal tubing, round which are whipped hair fibres from the tails of different animals. Orthodox salmon fly bodies are generally added to the tubes, and long-fibred hackles may be used in conjunction with the hair fibres, or even in place of them.

Tube Fly's history

The history of the tube fly is vague, and in fact there was at one time a great deal of discussion as to who was its originator. The history of the salmon fly itself has been dealt with in an earlier section, so it is sufficient to say that the tube fly is an extension of the traditional salmon fly, taking an evolutionary place in that history.

One of the first to reach the attention of salmon anglers was the Parker tube fly, since when all tube flies have followed a very similar style and method of construction. One of the earliest to earn a name was the Stoat Tail which, in its original form, consisted merely of fibres from the tail of a stoat, whipped round one end of a piece of tubing. As with all patterns which achieve a measure of popularity, variations soon began to appear, and these usually either took the form of additions to the tube body itself, using silk and tinsel as coverings, or by additions of different coloured hairs to those used on the original Stoat Tail.

Heron breast and guinea fowl body feathers are good examples of the feathers which are now used for tying tube flies, as

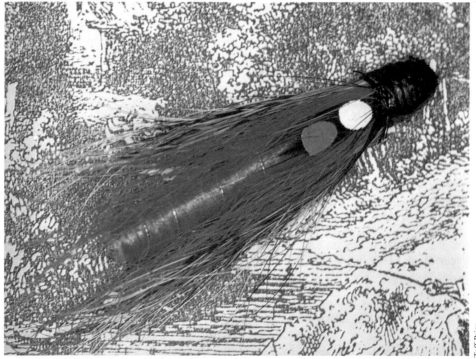

Taff Price

88

Taff Price

Taff Price

Tube running free
along leader

Treble
Hook

Rod Sutterby

*(Above A Stoat-Tail tube
fly still lodged in the vee of the
salmon's jaws.*
(Right) The basic tube fly.
*(Left) Squirrel and Orange
tube fly with eye spots painted
on the head.*

they have long, flowing fibres which work
well in the water when the fly is fished. Some
tubes are made of brass in which a polythene
tube has been inserted, thus giving weight for
deep water fishing without creating too
much wear and tear on the leader.

A double advantage
The tubes are used in conjunction with a
treble hook which is tied to the end of the
leader. The tube is then slid down the leader
tail-end first, until it is stopped by the eye of
the treble hook. From this you will see that
the tube is running free on the leader, a factor
which has a double advantage. When the fly
is being fished, the pressure of water holds it
tight to the treble hook, whereas when the
hook is taken by a fish the reverse applies,
and the drag caused by the fish's run drives
the tube up the leader towards the line. This
prevents damage to tube and dressing.

For colour variations or for increased size,
two made-up tubes may be used together and
two appropriate methods are illustrated.

Conventional fly tying equipment can be
used to make tube flies, plus one or two sizes
of tapered, eyeless salmon hooks on which
the tubes can be slid to facilitate tying. Hook
sizes 4, 2, 2/0 and 4/0 should cope with most
tube diameters. There is also a device,
designed by Anne Douglas, which fits into a
normal vice clamp and which has several
sizes of spike set onto an axle at the top. The
size needed is turned to the right of the stem
intended to take the tube while the other
sizes are turned left out of the way.

To prevent the treble from hanging at an
angle to the tube during casting, a small piece
of cycle valve rubber, or another short piece
of polythene tubing, can be fixed over the
hook end of each tube when it is completed.
The eye of the treble can then be drawn into
it before you start to fish. Unless you take
this precaution, the hook can snag itself on
the leader in front of the tube, resulting in a
large number of useless casts.

The Hairy Mary tube fly, chosen here for
step-by-step demonstration of tying, is a very
well-known tube adaptation, being a hair-

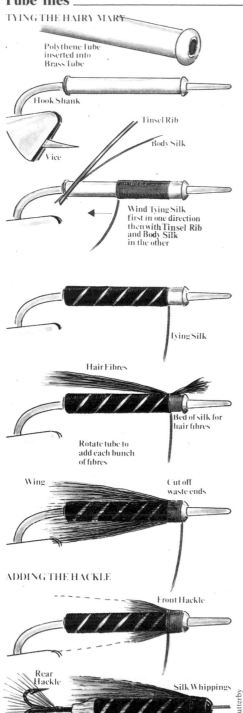

TYING THE HAIRY MARY

Polythene Tube
inserted into
Brass Tube

Hook Shank

Tinsel Rib

Body Silk

Vice

Wind Tying Silk
first in one direction
then with Tinsel Rib
and Body Silk
in the other

Tying Silk

Hair Fibres

Bed of silk for
hair fibres

Rotate tube to
add each bunch
of fibres

Wing

Cut off
waste ends

ADDING THE HACKLE

Front Hackle

Rear
Hackle

Silk Whippings

Rubber
Cycle Valve

Clear Varnish

winged salmon fly in its original form, which in its turn was an adaptation of the Blue Charm—one of the best known and most popular flies in the salmon angler's fly box. It varied only in that the original feather wing of the Blue Charm was replaced by brown bucktail (deer) fibres. The original tail tag, body and hackle ingredients were left intact.

Tying a Hairy Mary

To tie a Hairy Mary, first press the tube onto the tapered hook shank, firmly enough to hold it well but taking care not to split or damage the end of it. The bend of the hook is then held in the vice and tying silk run down the tube. Body silk and tinsel rib are tied in where the tail end of the fly would usually be. Wind the tying silk back the other way and follow it with the body silk and tinsel rib, in that order. Now put a layer of the tying silk on the remaining piece of tubing to form a bed for the ends of the hair fibres which are to be added.

The wing of the Hairy Mary is made from brown bucktail or, in the smaller patterns,

Rod Sutterby

squirrel tail. The best fibres for small tube flies, whichever kind of tail is used, will be found at the base, and for larger flies the fibres should be taken from whatever part of the tail suits them best, so that for very large flies the fibres would be from the tip. This makes best possible use of any variegated colour in the tail.

The hairs are cut off by twisting a small bunch of them together, and trimming them close to the root. Any fluffy fur—found at the base of most hair fibres—should be pricked out with the point of a dubbing needle: this fur has no use in the wing and only makes the finished head thicker than it need be. The size of the head should be kept to a minimum to prevent a bow-wave and speed entry into the water.

Do not try to put on too many hairs at a time: a good measure of quantity is their thickness when they are twisted together. The maximum, even for large flies, is a thickness of about $\frac{1}{16}$ in. The bunch of fibres is now tied in on top of the tube, making the

loop of tying silk over the fingers as you might for tying-in normal wings.

The waste ends should be cut off now and after each bunch of fibres is tied in. This makes for precision in each ensuing stage of the tying-in, whereas a large bunch of splayed-out waste fibres would obscure the head of the tube.

The tube is now rolled round the hook shank, bringing to the top the next portion which is to be covered by hairs. Another bunch of fibres is now tied in, the turns of silk being to the immediate right of those turns securing the first bunch. Continue in this way until the whole tube has been covered.

Keep the head small

Placing the silk turns to the right as each bunch is tied in will keep down the size of the head. If all the turns were in one place it would be quite bulky. Try to fix the 'steps' of tying silk so that the last bunch of fibres is completed just as the end of the tube is reached. A single layer of silk is wound round all the fibres where they are tied in. This forms a neat head and gives a uniform slope to the fibres. All the waste ends of the fibres were cut off as the body progressed, so that all that is now needed is a whip finish and one or two coats of thin clear varnish—Cellire is ideal—to the head. The silk whippings should be soaked well in the varnish for strength, and when dry, a final coat of black or red, as desired, completes the fly—apart from the addition of the hook.

If the tube fly requires a hackle in front, this is wound at the point where the first bunch of fibres was tied in. Using the fingers of your left hand, all the hackle fibres are drawn to the rear. Wind a few turns of silk over their base so that they contain the hair as closely as possible. Body hackles can be added as with a normal fly.

If heron hackles are used in the place of hair, one hackle is wound at the front and all its fibres pulled to the rear. On a larger pattern, it can be wound 'Palmer'-style.

Taff Price

Two kinds of body hackle (in blue) used on the Hairy Mary tube fly.

Sea trout flies

The life cycle of the sea trout is almost the same as that of the salmon, with the important difference that whereas salmon do not feed in freshwater, sea trout perhaps occasionally do. Consequently, when tying flies to tempt the sea trout, try to offer them something appetizing as well as attractive.

The first flies to concentrate on are those that represent the sea trout's main diet while at sea—small fish. These are still uppermost in its mind when it enters freshwater. Sea trout also feed on prawns, shrimps, sandeels, and small crabs, but small fish ranging from ½in–3in constitute its main diet.

There are several established patterns that are always worth a place in the fly box. Teal Blue and Silver is one of the most successful the author has come across, and it should be tied in sizes of 10 or 12 through to long-shanked flies or tandem lures of up to 3in.

Other successful flies are Peter Ross, Silver Wilkinson, Teal and Red, Mallard and Silver, Mallard and Gold, and other bright patterns, all tied in the styles described to imitate small fish.

'Medicines'

One of the greatest authorities on sea trout fishing is Hugh Falkus. In his book *Sea Trout Fishing* he gives details of seven types of sea trout fly to suit different conditions. The first kind, which he calls 'Medicines', are effective all night but are best fished before midnight. They are big silver/blue patterns such as the Silver Blue or the Mallard and Silver, and are tied very lightly on low water salmon hooks. These are longer-shanked and lighter in the wire than normal hooks.

The second group, 'Sunk Lures', are good late night flies. They consist of two size 8 or 10 short-shanked hooks tied in tandem. The

Arthur Oglesby

(Left) A big sunk lure, a small sea trout fly with flying treble, and a small sea trout fly.
(Below) Sea trout versions of the Silver Wilkinson and the March Brown. There are various patterns of these well-known artificials.

MARCH BROWN

Lyn Cawley

SILVER WILKINSON

ZULU

CONNEMARA

Lyn Cawley

(Above) The Zulu and the Connemara, two flies known to attract sea trout. (Right) The 'Medicine', created and named by a great fisherman, Brigadier G H N Wilson. It is tied on low-water salmon hooks, sizes 3, 4 or 5.

overall length of the lure should be about 2½in. The wings are constructed of blue hackle feathers, strands of peacock herl, or blue-dyed fur. No hackles are wound in front of these lures, nor do they have tails. In fact, Falkus states that tails are unnecessary on most sea trout flies.

The third group, 'Maggot Flies', is a well-established method of sea trout fishing, and the pattern recommended by Falkus is: hook, short-shanked and snecked; body, white thread or silk; hackle, brown hen. Use these flies in conjunction with two or three maggots fixed to the bend of the hook.

Fourth is Falkus's specially constructed pattern—the 'Secret Weapon'. These flies are designed to overcome the frustration caused by fish that are 'taking short', nibbling at the end of the bait without getting near the hook. Their secret is a flying treble extending beyond the bend (and parallel to the wings) of a normally baited maggot fly.

Falkus lists two other flies. The 'Small Double', consists of a size 12 double-iron

hook, silver body, teal or mallard wing, and a black hen hackle. It is recommended when the fish are in a finicky mood in low water. The other lure, the 'Worm Fly', consists of a peacock herl body, about 1¼in–1½in long, with brown or black hen hackles. It is very good in low water, fished in tandem.

'Surface Lure'

Falkus's final lure, the 'Surface Lure', merits special attention. It is a dark-night lure which is quickly dragged across the surface. It can be made of almost anything that floats as it is not the fly itself but the wake that attracts the trout, although it is normally constructed from a piece of trimmed cork about 1½in long. This is whipped to a tandem mount of a leading single and a rear treble hook. The fly is then adorned with two wings of small, dark feathers.

Sea trout continue to feed after entering freshwater. As the season progresses other types of flies, representing freshwater food, can be used with success. Such patterns as 'March Brown', 'March Brown Silver',

'SECRET WEAPON' MOUNT

Wind on a few turns of silk (red) as a seating. Loop 12lb nylon round a No 16 treble and pass the ends out through the eye.

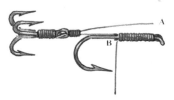

Whip nylon to shank and whip nylon together above eye.

Hold size 8 Hardy Perfect in vice and take a few turns of silk from opposite hook point to eye. Cut off end A just behind eye. Bring end B through eye and back along underside of shank. Whip back towards point tying in strand B.

Wind silk back towards eye, this time trapping end A. Whip finish. Ensure eye of the treble is level with bend of hook.

Add sparse wing of mallard and a black cock or hen hackle for dressing.

Rod Sutterby

'Invicta', 'Mallard and Claret', 'Butcher', and 'Zulu' all catch fish. Double hooks are useful when the fish are in a fussy mood.

The size of a fly is more important than its shape, and a great deal depends on the weather and water conditions. Standard patterns should be about size 8–10 under normal conditions, with 6–8 being used on windy days. Colour is also important. Dark flies are best in waters with dark, rocky bottoms, such as Irish lakes and rivers, and suggested patterns for these conditions are 'Black Pennell', 'Connemara Black', 'Butcher', and 'Black Zulu'. If you fish a team of three flies, the 'Black Pennell' seems to be the most successful as the tail fly on any water, although the body should be varied in colour from time to time. Use claret or yellow for example, but always with plenty of bright silver or gold ribbing.

Whether to use a large fish imitation or a smaller freshwater fly depends largely on the season. In the early season you may well

adopt the maxim that a big fly will catch more fish than a small fly used at the same time in the same water. But the longer a fish stays in a river on its return from the sea, the more is it likely to return to the food available in its new environment. As its instinct for sea food fades, it will turn to the nymphs and flies found in freshwater.

Learn the feeding habits

Having learnt the feeding habits of sea trout, the angler who ties his own flies has all the advantages. He can make lures resembling small fish, as he knows them to be and which are not the creation of someone else's imagination (very often that someone has never fished for sea trout in his life), and flies that represent the insect life in the particular water he fishes. With his own individually designed flies he is far more likely to succeed. One of the author's friends had six sea trout on one outing, the largest 11lb. All were taken on a 'Teal Blue and Silver' of his own design, tied on very long shanked hooks, very sparsely and with no tails, the wing being of widgeon feather, not the usual teal.

(Above) A selection of sea trout flies including Teal and Blue, Mallard and Claret, Alexandra, Peter Ross, Woodcock and Yellow, and Silver March Brown.
(Right) A surface fly in the muddler minnow style.
(Below) The best standard sea trout lure, the worm fly.
(Far left) How to tie the famous 'Secret Weapon' sea trout fly. The lure was designed in 1962.

WORM FLY

Fly boxes

The only criterion by which to judge a good fly box is whether it caters for your needs, whether it holds all the flies that your particular brand of fishing demands. In my case this adds up to several thousand, and although this may sound unnecessary, I would hate to leave any of them behind. But each angler asks something different of a fly box, and this article can aim only to introduce the various categories of box along with a few specific models.

The firm of Richard Wheatley has been making fly boxes of all types for a considerable time, and have satisfied the needs of many fishermen. The No. 1601 model from the Wheatley range is fitted with small metal clips on both sides and will hold 119 flies. On one side of the box there are large clips for the bigger flies and on the other, small clips for your nymphs and smaller patterns. The whole box is neat, will fit into most pockets, and is light, being made from aluminium.

Held by the hooks

There are other boxes in this range, some with an extra flap inside to hold even more hooks, as well as boxes that will take salmon flies, gripping them by the hooks. This method of securing the flies may be considered unsatisfactory because it spoils the hackles—which in these days are hard to come by. So Wheatleys have produced a different design in model No 1607F which incorporates a neat, hinged, sprung lid to each compartment. By simply flicking the catch on each lid, it springs open revealing the flies soundly protected inside. The box has 16 compartments with sprung lids and should hold 80 to 100 dry flies. In size it is only slightly thicker then the previous box. Another model has compartments on both sides and, while quite expensive, it is a first-class box for the really keen dry fly man.

Without a doubt, for the man who likes to travel light, the best value for money is John Goddard's box marketed by Efgeeco. This

box will answer all your needs if you are content to carry only a small selection of flies to the waterside safe and in good condition and leave the larger boxes behind. The box is made from a very durable plastic lined with polythene foam which acts to stop hooks rusting. It will hold about 140 flies and is very light to carry as you walk your favourite chalk-stream. The designer recommends the box—by using it himself.

To get away from shop-bought boxes, you can make all manner of containers if you are

P. H. Ward/Tackle Carrier Watford

P. H. Ward/Tackle Carrier Watford

The Wheatley box (below left) holds flies under spring clips; Efgeeco's box (left) keeps the flies firmly in rows; (above) this box, again by Wheatley, has eight compartments.

Irish Tourist Board

at all 'DIY' minded. A wooden cigar box is often put to good use in this way. The first step is to take any paper off the outside and give the whole thing—including the inside— a good rub down with a medium sandpaper. Put two or three coats of varnish on the outside to make the box waterproof. Next, get some polythene foam from your tackle shop.

If you line the box with white Fablon before you stick the foam in, it seems to help make the flies stand out more clearly, especially when you are searching for one particular pattern at night. You can either put a complete layer of foam in the top and bottom or cut the foam into strips and stick them into the box, depending on whether you want to keep just lures in the box or hackle flies as well.

Protecting hackles

A box which answers this description is available commercially from Benwoods of London. Handmade by a skilled tool-maker, it is made from wood and lined with Fablon. Polythene foam is stuck into it in narrow strips so that the hackles of flies do not get damaged. (This can happen when the whole inside of a box has been lined with foam.) It is a model which the author recommends.

A recent box to come onto the market is the Gripstrip fly box. Normark manufacture and sell the box along with a free Adaptaleader. (This 16ft knotless tapered cast should fill a long-felt want in the leader market.) The method of holding flies is quite revolutionary; it consists of hundreds of tiny nylon fibres gripped at one end in a metal strip. Two of these strips face each other, the loose ends of the fibres facing. A fly is secured simply by pushing it in between the nylon fibre-tips.

They seem to grip the flies very well; they do not fall out even when the box is banged forcibly. It is most important that flies should not shake loose from the device holding them because otherwise you will regularly open the box to find your flies in a tangled heap.

This is the great disadvantage of the magnetic styles of fly box. When dropped, the flies shake loose from the magnetic strips or the sheet of rubber-coated magnetized metal which lines this kind of box. In addition, the sheet-magnet design tends to bend fly hackles drastically out of shape. For these reasons, the magnetic box cannot be strongly recommended.

The next box can be worth every penny of its small cost. The box consists of six separate compartments, three on each side, with a sprung lid. It is manufactured in clear, strong plastic and holds a good quantity of flies. It is particularly useful for river fishing when, if you know your river well, you can select the most 'likely' flies for the conditions, and leave the bigger stock of flies behind in their cumbersome boxes. An additional asset is a small ring on one end so that it can be attached to a waistcoat. These cheap, imported boxes are definitely value for money, and your local tackle dealer will probably have such a product in stock.

Selection of fly boxes

When buying fly boxes, decide in advance exactly what you require; whether you want all your flies stored together or whether you want to keep the various kinds separate. Several small boxes can help if you are trying to develop ranges of the same type of fly, e.g. wool-bodied, seal's fur or floss-bodied buzzer nymphs. A collection of flies in a good assortment of sizes will need plenty of room if they are to stay neat.

If you buy a box that has a lot of metal inside, keep the box as dry as possible when fishing—otherwise you will find that all your carefully tied flies have rusted. You should also check the box to make sure that it is as waterproof as possible and would float if dropped into water at any time.

(Left) Flies can quickly become tangled.
(Below left) Nymph and wet fly collection.
(Below) The standing box is made so that nylon fibres grip the hooks securely.

Mike Prichard

Irish Tourist Board

D. Laffin/Benwoods

Gaffs and tailers

The task of lifting a fish from the water and landing it safely on the bank can, in the vast majority of cases, be accomplished with a net. But a net large enough to lift a heavy fish from the water makes quite an encumbrance if it is to be carried across the shoulder or trailed from place to place by the lone angler. There are two alternatives to using the net: one is the gaff, the other a tailer. Both are lightweight, sure and convenient; each possesses disadvantages that need careful consideration before purchase.

For many anglers, especially pike fishermen, a gaff has become a status symbol which shows that the owner means business and intends to land big fish. Unfortunately, they use the gaff on every fish that is caught, regardless of size, and have no qualms about returning such fish, despite any wound that has been inflicted. Worse still, many of the gaffs that are used would be quite inadequate to deal with a very big fish.

Collapsible or telescopic gaffs seem to be most popular. They range from lightweight

Arthur Oglesby

alloy to heavy models. Those made from alloy cost less but tend to corrode over the years, often resulting in their joints sticking when extended. Light oiling helps smooth running, but will not cure minor dents and distortions that so easily occur when using handles made of soft alloy.

Protecting gaff heads

Good quality gaffs have steel or heavy gauge brass sections with a firm rubber or cork handle, and the added safety precaution of a leather thong that can be looped over the wrist. Even if this is not fitted to the gaff when purchased, it can be easily added. Gaff heads are invariably made from steel, and should be kept oiled.

(Previous page) Pity the gaff has to be used here but perhaps a tailer was not to hand. The salmon is an autumn fish, taken on the Yorkshire Esk near Whitby.
(Below) Tackling up, with the effective tailer standing ready for action.

Bill Howes

Much is written about sharpening the point of a gaff at regular intervals, but if the point is adequately protected, this should not be necessary other than at the beginning of the season. Protection should be in the form of a brass safety cup into which the point will fit, and not a loose piece of cork haphazardly pushed onto the point.

The gape, or distance between the point of the gaff and its shank, is vitally important. Too little and it will be impossible to draw the point home; too much will effect balance and cause the handle to turn in use.

Fixed gaffs consist of a wooden pole to which a head is firmly screwed and then close-whipped with copper wire. It can be carried bandolier-style across the shoulders by a cord, clipping just below the waist with a spring clip that allows immediate release. Many anglers construct their own with a large sea hook and a broom handle—a practical approach provided that a large-enough hook is used. A tope hook is only just big enough and conger hooks are worse than useless. Every trace of the barb must be removed and any sneck, or offset angle, at the bend should be straightened.

Correct use of the gaff

To gaff a fish once it is played out needs a steady hand and a lot of common sense. Movement made by the gaff as it approaches the fish will often cause the creature to lunge away, and all temptation to strike at the fish should be resisted at that critical moment. Only when the fish is lying prone on the surface should the point be introduced, and then at the point of the jaw, where there is likely to be less movement than along the stomach or shoulder.

Once the point is well home, the fish should be lifted straight onto the bank in a single movement, taking care to lift with the handle and shift held vertically. A horizontal lift will throw an enormous strain on the handle and is the prime cause of gaffs bending and distorting. Several steps should be taken away from the water's edge before any move to release the fish—many premature struggles result in a fish's escape.

Bill Howes

Used properly, with a sharp rap, the priest kills cleanly and quickly.

While the gaff relies on penetration in order to land the fish, the tailer uses a grip around the 'wrist,' just before the caudal fin, to hold and lift a fish onto the bank. Its business end consists of a heavy length of stiff, cabled steel, bent and held open by a thin, flexible wire that connects to the handle. When the fish is played out, the open wire loop is slid over the tail and back onto the 'wrist' immediately before the caudal fin.

How to use the tailer

Once in place the handle of the tailer is raised sharply; the wire noose will immediately clamp tightly into the flesh, rather like a snare around a rabbit's neck. The fish can be lifted clear of the water by the same vertical lift that would be used with a gaff.

The advantage of a tailer is that, with sensible use, an undersized or out-of-season fish can be released with little or no damage—something that is impossible when a gaff has been used. But there is one annoying disadvantage in the tailer, and that

is the tendency of the trip wire that holds the loop open to slip off its support every time it is knocked, closing the noose. The device needs constantly to be reset.

Killing a fish should be carried out as quickly and humanely as possible. Most anglers realize that the easiest way is to strike the head with a heavy object, but often this simple action is carried to extremes and anglers are seen using large pieces of wood, bottles, and even kicks from an angler's heavy boot to despatch the fish. Incidents like this are fuel for the anti-blood sport lobby, and as likely to bring discredit to the sport as leaving a fish to die on the bank.

The humane priest

For a very small price it is possible to purchase a priest—a short length of weighted wood, metal or horn, that can apply the final stroke neatly and humanely—hence the angling expression 'visited by the priest'. Two or three firm blows across the top of the head, behind the eyes, and the dead fish is ready for wrapping in the damp leaves or rushes that will keep it fresh until it is time for cooking or storing in a deep freeze.

101

Clothing

The fisherman should not select clothes in order to look attractive. He wants hard wear, warmth, and water-proofing. He needs clothes that can stand up to barbed wire, thorny foliage, and the worst the weather can throw at him. Colours should be subdued, even camouflaged.

Even so it is difficult to resist the romance and sheer snob appeal of clothes specially designed for golfers, campers, mountaineers and yachtsmen which are displayed in the sportswear shops. A glance at the garish colours and fancy buttons, however, usually stops the angler being caught, and the thought of flying drawstrings and toggles tangled with fishing line should drive him out of the shop in a near panic.

Perhaps it is time anglers stopped using old clothes for fishing as they are a pretty scruffy-looking lot. Maybe they should change their image, and if you feel that way there is plenty of high-quality clothing specially designed by anglers for anglers. It is not available in the sportswear shops, but local tackle dealers have a wide range.

A good jacket

The priority is a good jacket, and this must be comfortable and warm. It should be a size larger than the best tailor would recommend, so that it has space for an extra sweater underneath without making the arms uncomfortable.

At its best, and if you can afford it, it should be waterproof with a strong zip-fastener which can unzip from the top and from the bottom. This should be covered with a press-fastened flap. Ideally it should have storm pockets and elastic wrist fittings under roomy sleeves and cuffs, with well-designed ventilation holes under the arms. A wide turn-up collar is preferable, and valuable optional extras are a clip-on hood, and a stud-fastened inner lining, both of which can be fitted or discarded at will. Several well-known manufacturers produce this kind of garment, and they are made in both lightweight and heavyweight fabrics. Some offer an optional lining.

Other jackets are designed only to be shower-proof. These are cheaper, and if that is all you need then they are excellent. In heavy rain a lightweight over-mac can be worn, and if it fits in the pocket when not in use it makes a good alternative kit.

There are two basic waterproof materials available. The old-established oiled silk or cotton has stood the test of time. It retains its water resistance for years, but usually needs cleaning and re-proofing at intervals of up to five years. It has only two minor faults. In very cold weather it goes stiff as a board and may cut into your neck unless a scarf is worn, and when wet fly fishing the oil may soak on to the cast, preventing it from sinking properly. The more recently manufactured

heavy-duty kapok-lined nylon jacket or anorak is snug and warm in a boat in mid-winter and with its detachable lining it can be light and windproof on milder days.

Match fishermen tend to favour the shower-proof jacket with an ultra-light plastic or nylon portable overjacket which rolls up and fits easily in a pocket. They rely chiefly on their umbrellas for protection from the rain, but they also use waterproof over-trousers, which take the suffering out of sitting on a wet seat and protect the legs and thighs from the rain that cascades off plastic macs. Anyone who fishes from a boat regularly would also find these valuable.

Matching 'accessories'

(Above) Jack Lucas, the well-dressed game fisherman with three brace of good trout. (Below) Fly casting on the Dee from a rock, but well prepared to wade waist-deep.

For 'matching accessories' most anglers still rely on the old fashioned string-vest under a heavy twill or cotton shirt to retain inner warmth. The ex-serviceman's long woollen underpants might raise a laugh from friends in the hotel in the evening, but they are well worth it for the warmth they provide. Gloves are essential but not always effective—cold

Irish Tourist Board

fingers are something to which the angler must steel himself against, or stay at home when it's frosty. Mittens are an excellent compromise which enable tackle to be managed easily and at the same time reduce the cold.

The angler's waistcoat is popular with most people. It is invaluable for carrying disgorgers and forceps, scissors and shots and a host of other small equipment for which you would otherwise have to rummage in the tackle bag.

One universally popular garment is the angler's hat. Fashions keep changing, but what really matters is the protection it offers in a sport where hooks are thrown about willy-nilly. Polaroid sun glasses are an extra protection from other people's flying hooks and from the glare off the water.

Footwear

Finally, footwear is important. Anyone who has walked long distances in wellingtons or waders without proper understockings hardly needs to be told that thick sea-boot stockings or something similar are essential. So your footwear must be a size larger than usual to accommodate them. This also allows some ventilation space and helps keep feet warm. Most waders have press-stud and strap fittings at the knee which enable them

The sun may be shining, but lough fishing in Ireland demands that the angler be ready for any emergency the weather can bring.

to be folded down and worn 'Buccaneer' fashion. This is useful when walking between swims, and especially when sitting on a boat where the creases under the knees are uncomfortable.

Whatever footwear you choose the soles must be suitable for your kind of fishing. If you fish off concrete, or scramble over or wade in rocky hard-bottomed waters you must have metal-studded leather soles. Rubber is slippery and almost suicidal. For reservoirs and grassy banks and generally soft-bottomed waters composition plastic soles are excellent provided they have a deep tread. Once the tread has gone they become extremely dangerous and should be thrown out immediately.

Clothing is still very much a matter of personal choice and preference according to the kind of fishing you do, but warmth and comfort certainly provide the confidence and concentration which enable you to fish successfully. Attractive appearance might help in the local pub at lunch time, but on the bank only the fish can benefit, and if they see you first then you are wasting your time.

Arthur Ogelsley

Basic flycasting

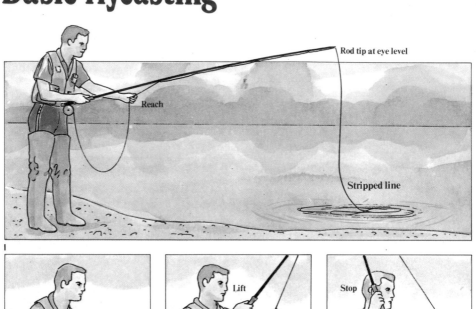

Rod tip at eye level

Reach

Stripped line

1

Pull

2

Lift

3

Stop

4

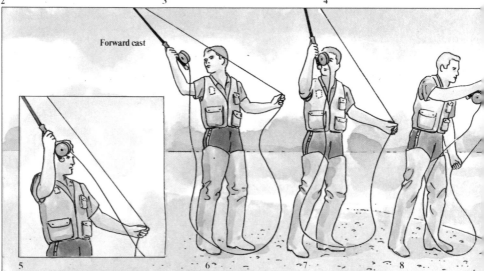

Forward cast

5

6

7

8

The technique of fly casting was described by Izaak Walton like this: 'In casting your line, do it always before you, so that your fly may, first, fall upon the water and as little of your line with it, as is possible'. This advice, in *The Compleat Angler*, is as true today as it was in 1653. The aim is to present the artificial fly to the fish in as natural a way as possible. This means that it must alight on the water in imitation of the natural insect, creating that small spreading ripple which induces the fish to take. But fly casting is a practical skill, very difficult to illustrate as a single, flowing motion. It is not a difficult skill to learn once the basic requirements are understood.

The basic problem

It is important to understand that there is only one basic problem and therefore only one real mistake to be made in fly casting.

The problem is that you must make the fly rod do the work, and not your arm. The rod must be made to act as a spring in order to propel a virtually weightless object, the fly, through the air. The function of the spring is to store up energy, and then release it when required. This can be understood in terms of two simple arm movements, which are equivalent to the loading and unloading of the spring.

The back cast

The action of fly casting, simply described, is that the line is lifted from the water by the rod and briskly thrown back behind the caster. This is called the 'back cast'. There is a pause while the line streams out and straightens behind the caster, who prevents the rod from straying back beyond the vertical by thumb pressure on the top of the handle. In that essential pause, the line, while streaming out behind the caster, is also pulling back the rod tip, making the whole rod flex. The rod and line are then driven forward again on the 'forward cast'. This flexing of the rod is the equivalent of a spring being wound up.

The base of the spring, in this case, is the butt of the rod. As with all springs, the base has to be locked firmly, or its energy will leak away The locking action is achieved by the

The accumulated energy in the spring of the rod drives the line forward in the most graceful action to be found in fishing.

Try to achieve a smooth motion, first of the back cast then the forward cast.
(1) The angler strips about six yards of line from the reel and works it through the rod rings. (2) The back cast begins as the rod is held with the tip roughly at eye level and then lifted sharply upwards (3), with the left hand ensuring that the line is not pulled through the rings by the surface tension of the water. (4) The back cast continues to (5), where the position of the thumb should ensure that the rod does not go too far back beyond the vertical. As it stops, the spring of the rod will act to store energy for the forward cast. With the rod at full tension (6) the forward cast can begin (7), energy stored in the spring of the rod being released (8).

Rod Sutterby

'stopping' of the wrist at the point when the rod butt is roughly level with the ear during the back cast. The wrist is locked and as it is dragged back by the power applied to the back cast and the weight of the pulling line, the rod is forced to flex.

Wrist movement

The role of the wrist is actually far more complex than this necessarily simplified description of a cast. Experienced fly casters use wrist movement and virtually nothing else to control the rod and line, both in basic overhead casting and in other kinds of cast, to be described in later issues. Beginners should concentrate on stopping the wrist from following the rod backwards, as it would naturally do. If this is allowed to happen energy will not be stored in the base of the rod. This means that the angler will have to compensate for the lack of energy in the rod by applying extra muscular power to the forward cast. This in turn will lead to a weak or lazy back cast, simply because it becomes unnecessary to have a strong one.

Maximum results

Correctly done, fly casting will seem to require little effort or have little power behind it but will have maximum results, that is, the angler will be able to cast a long way without feeling tired. It is correct to say

that if the casting arm is tired after half an hour, then there is something wrong with the angler's casting technique.

Use the spring—not force

Really good fly-line casters are extremely rare, and the gap between the standard of their performance and that of the average fly fisherman is enormous. Many fly fishermen with years of experience do not use their fly-rod as a spring. They use force instead, but nevertheless believe that they are casting correctly because they can send the line some distance. In Britain there seems to be very little interest in casting as a separate, important part of fly fishing. There are fly-tying clubs but casting clubs usually fail for lack of support. Most anglers seem reluctant to learn from an expert and seem quite happy to go on casting in a haphazard fashion.

Importance of lessons

It is important to have several lessons with a professional instructor as this allows the student to gain a natural technique based on direct observation.

The technique of fly casting has been shown many times as a series of frozen poses, each one illustrating where the angler's arm, wrist, or the line, should be at a given moment. But it must be stressed that the action of the fly rod and line is a fluid motion

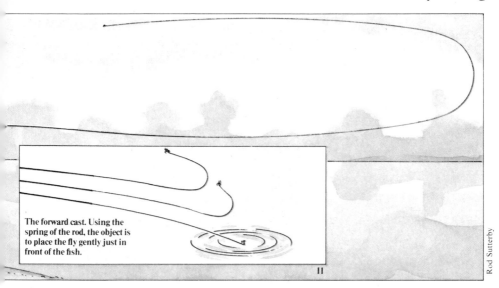

The forward cast. Using the spring of the rod, the object is to place the fly gently just in front of the fish.

II

Rod Sutterby

which should comprise one graceful arm movement. Any errors picked up and not corrected immediately by a teacher could easily become a habit. If you practise the wrong technique several times and become used to it, it will be very hard to correct later. Rather than focusing on the errors and trying to correct them one at a time, you would probably have to start from the beginning again, because the process must be learnt as a whole rather than broken up into stages. It is a mistaken approach to teach or learn such a technique on the basis of correcting errors, since concentrating on only one small part of the casting routine will cause it to lose its fluidity and be broken up.

The object: to catch fish

In spite of its importance as a technique to be mastered, casting is a means to catch fish, and not an end in itself. Where the fly lands on the water is an essential part of the skill: for example, successful reservoir fishing often depends on the ability to throw a very long line. But wherever you fish, accuracy of casting is vital. Right from the beginning of your tuition in fly casting, aim to reach the fish. Accuracy will enable you to do that.

Like life in general, bad habits are hard to correct. So start as you mean to go on—with good habits.

(Above) The forward cast continues (from previous page). When the pull through the rod rings is felt by the left hand, the line is released to shoot through, allowing the line to unfurl. As the line straightens out the angler lowers the rod horizontally, allowing the line to meet the water gently. (Inset) Properly cast, the fly touches the water exactly like a natural fly alighting. (Below) A fly casting demonstration. The forward cast is nearly completed.

Bill Howes

Arthur Ogelsley

Roll and spey casts

Despite what some people say and what is written about fly casting, it is a comparatively easy operation. Nevertheless, it is one that makes all the difference between enjoying fishing and not becoming fatigued at the end of the day, or becoming frustrated or tired, possibly losing many flies and fish.

The first essential is to understand what happens when a rod loaded with the correct weight of line is turned through an arc from a horizontal position to the vertical, held for a slight pause and then returned to the horizontal. This is the basic casting action and can be adjusted to give various types of cast, but each must have the same pendulum action from the rod handle.

As the rod is turned through its arc, it acts as a spring being wound up and then, as the spring unwinds, it transmits power to the piece of line at its end. This section of line then starts travelling forward and as it does so gradually turns over until it has completely unfolded and straightened out the rest of the length of line. This is only possible because a tapered line decreases in weight per unit length and each reduced weight portion is able to be moved by a decreased amount of energy. The energy is, of course, decreasing all the time from the moment the rod has imparted its energy to the line.

Three simple steps

To go a step farther, and smooth out the line, consider the movement to be in three parts. To do this, visualize a clock between nine and twelve. For the back cast, start with the rod in the nine o'clock position. Raise the rod slowly to eleven o'clock—this movement will lift most of the line from the water. The wrist then comes into action, accelerating the sweep of the rod and propelling the line backwards. During the wrist action the forearm still continues its stroke. This power stage must never carry on past the twelve o'clock position. The rod, however, may be allowed to travel beyond the vertical position, provided that it is merely drifting and that all the power has been cut off completely. At this point the rod must be held stationary for a brief pause in order to allow the line time to fully extend behind. The length of pause depends upon the length of line being cast and the wind conditions.

The forward cast is a repeat of the lift or back cast, but in the opposite direction. From the vertical the rod is moved slowly at first, then, when it reaches the eleven o'clock position, the wrist again accelerates the movement until ten o'clock, when the power is cut off and the rod is followed through (i.e. drifted) to nine o'clock.

Roll cast

By the time you have progressed with the basic mechanics of casting and can cast a line into the air behind you, allow it to straighten out and then reverse the procedure, casting a quiet, straight line onto the water where you want it, you should then be able to make the roll cast.

In some cases it is necessary to fish with some obstruction such as trees or perhaps a very high bank behind you, which rules out a normal overhead back cast. But it need not prevent you fishing in this particular stretch of water, and it is in such places that one can very often catch more fish as the inexpert caster will avoid this part of the river and always fish where he can make a conventional back cast. To cast under such conditions calls for the slightly different technique of the roll cast.

In this cast the line never goes behind the caster's body and never leaves the water. In order to create the weight (i.e. the pull of line against the rod) required to bend the rod into its loaded form, the friction of the line on the water in front of the caster is used. To perform this cast, the rod point is raised very slowly right up to one o'clock and held there until the line bellies to such a position that the extreme point of its curve is roughly in line with the caster's back. When the line reaches this position, a normal forward cast is made with a little more effort than usual, and the rod point is carried on down almost onto the water—in other words, instead of the power being cut off at approximately ten o'clock, it is carried on right through past nine o'clock, and in this particular cast there is no follow-through. This may sound difficult, but in fact is very easy indeed when it is tried out and these simple points are remembered.

The power stroke

One such point is that when making a roll cast the line must always be clear of itself and the cast must never be attempted in such a way that the line which rolls out will go over the line which is already on the water at the beginning of the power stroke. The following simple rule explains this more clearly: when you intend to roll your line to a point to the right of where it already lies on the water, it must be brought up during the backwards slow lift to a position at the *left* side of the rod. When the line is to be cast to a position to the left of where it already lies then the line must be brought up slowly to a point to the *right* of the rod. If this rule is followed the line is always going away from itself and never tangles.

In some cases a strong side wind may be blowing against the caster, which could blow the line into a position in which it might foul. Under these conditions, the rod must be laid over more to the side during the backward slow-lifting stroke, but it must be remembered before the normal power stroke is carried out that the rod must be raised to the

vertical position and cast forward in a vertical plane.

Spey cast

Where the roll cast is useful in trout fishing with a single-handed rod, the Spey cast comes into its own in salmon fishing with a double-handed rod for fishing down tree-lined river banks.

The basic difference between the roll and Spey casts is that in the simple roll cast the line never leaves the water, while in the Spey, the line is completely lifted from the water and dropped back again in a new position from where a roll cast can be made. The cast is made in the same way as the simple roll

A demonstration of the roll cast by a past expert. The late Tommy Edwards, on the Spey, showing how the cast should be made.

Arthur Oglesby

cast. It is the pre-positioning of the line which creates a difference.

The timing of the Spey cast is extremely critical (more so than in any other type of cast) and this makes it the most difficult cast of all to do properly.

Consider making a Spey cast from the left bank of a river: it is desirable to have the right hand at the top of the rod handle and the left hand at the bottom. At the same time, the right foot should be pointing forward.

Using the current

Having fished the fly around and into your own bank (i.e. in this instance the left bank) and having let it 'hang' in the current for a while immediately downstream in order to fully straighten the line out below you, the rod is first of all lowered to ensure a good clean lift.

Now, raise the rod straight up to the eleven o'clock position. The body and feet are not moved during this movement of the rod. This movement gets the line on to the surface of the water and in a position in readiness for the next part of the cast.

Placing line upstream

The next movement is fairly complex and involves the swivelling of the body and the transference of the line to a position upstream and to the right of the angler. He is now facing the new direction in which the cast is to be made.

Move the rod in a 'half-moon' curve from the eleven o'clock position to a one o'clock position upstream. During this movement it moves through 180° and at the same time goes from eleven o'clock to a horizontal position at 90° (i.e. half way) and back up again to the one o'clock position.

Acceleration

Because the rod is moved in a semi-circle it follows that the line comes round from in front of the caster to a position upstream. The movement of the rod is accelerated during the second half of the curve and as the rod is raised (from a horizontal position back up to one o'clock) the line is completely lifted off the water.

Now, the rod is arrested briefly, allowing

Roll and Spey casts

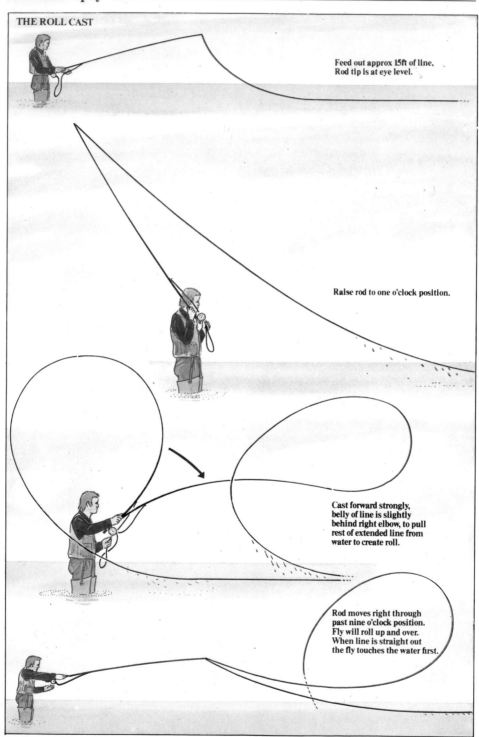

THE ROLL CAST

Feed out approx 15ft of line.
Rod tip is at eye level.

Raise rod to one o'clock position.

Cast forward strongly,
belly of line is slightly
behind right elbow, to pull
rest of extended line from
water to create roll.

Rod moves right through
past nine o'clock position.
Fly will roll up and over.
When line is straight out
the fly touches the water first.

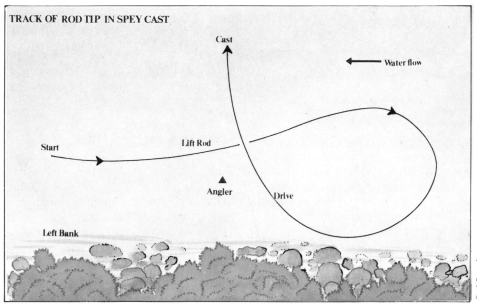

TRACK OF ROD TIP IN SPEY CAST

Cast

Water flow

Start · Lift Rod

Angler · Drive

Left Bank

Rod Sutterby

the line to drop on to the water. As soon as the line touches the water, the power is applied from the one o'clock position all the way through to about eight o'clock without any follow through. This motion is exactly that which is used in a simple roll cast.

While the 'half-moon' movement is being made the body must swivel from facing directly downstream to facing in a direction across the river in which the final delivery of the cast will be made.

After the lift of the rod from downstream and as the 'half-moon' curve is made, the body is swivelled by pivoting on the right heel and left toe to face the new direction. From this position the final execution of the cast can be made.

Critical timing of the Spey cast

The most critical part of the timing of the Spey cast is the pause while the line drops on to the water. If this is too long and as a consequence too much line lands on the water, the drag becomes too much and the line cannot be rolled out fully. If, on the other hand, insufficient line is on the water (because the pause has not been long enough) then the point of the line will flick into the air with a 'crack' and again the line

will not be rolled out as it should be.

The pause and the resulting length of line on the water can only be measured in parts of a second, so practice is essential in order to make a good Spey cast.

To make a Spey cast from the right bank, exactly the same movement is employed but the hands and feet are reversed.

Double Spey cast

If there is a very strong downstream wind blowing and this results in the line being blown under the rod, making the Spey cast difficult, the double Spey cast can be made. This cast (from the left bank of the river) is made with the hands and feet reversed; i.e. left hand up the handle and left foot forward.

In the first part of this cast the rod is taken upstream in an identical movement to the Spey cast. The line, however, is not dropped onto the water but is led back downstream with a 'half-moon' curve of the rod (without returning the body to face downstream). The line is dropped on to the water and the final delivery is made. Because the line is downstream the wind blows it away from the rod, allowing a cast to be made where otherwise it would be impossible.

Wet fly fishing

Wet fly fishing is, quite simply, the art of fishing an artificial fly beneath the surface of the water, either in imitation of a natural food item, or as an 'attractor'—a pattern which seems to bear no resemblance to any living creature but which induces a fish to strike at it in curiosity, anger or defence. Patterns referred to as 'nymphs' and 'bugs' usually attempt to imitate specific life forms, although there are more than a few patterns which bear a general resemblance to a number of different creatures and therefore are imitative of a range of natural forms, rather than one specific form.

Traditional wet flies

Traditional wet flies tend, very often, to fall into the 'attractor' category, bearing no close resemblance to anything in nature. There are others that do, nevertheless, imitate, either in colour or shape, living creatures such as small fry, or the pupal or larval forms of insects. Of the vast range of lures now available, some are designed to resemble small fry of all manner of species, while others merely suggest small fish by their outline and the way that they move in the water when retrieved correctly. It is probable, however, that the majority are neither shaped nor coloured like any small fish, and succeed in catching trout by the attractor principle.

'Point' and 'dropper' flies

The traditional version of wet fly fishing involves the use of a team of three flies, although, in times past, there are records of anglers using a dozen or more patterns at the same time. A modern wet fly leader has one fly attached to the end of the leader: this is the 'point' fly, and more often than not is a dressing tied to simulate a nymph or bug. Perhaps a yard above the point fly there is a 'dropper', a loose length of nylon projecting from the leader to which the second fly, also called a dropper, is attached. This often tends to be an attractor pattern, like a

Bloody Butcher, which some anglers believe to be recognized by the trout as a tiny minnow, or stickleback. A yard or so above the dropper, is another dropper, to which the 'bob' fly is tied. This usually tends to be a biggish, bushy dressing, such as a Zulu, or a Palmer, which bounces and bobs across the surface of the water during the retrieve.

Standard tactics when river fishing are to commence at the upstream end of the beat, casting upstream at an angle of 45°, allowing the line to sweep around with the current, and lifting off again when the line forms an angle of 45° downstream. After each retrieve, the angler moves a yard or so downstream and repeats the process. This is virtually the opposite of the dry fly fisherman's tactics, since he will normally prefer to work upstream, so it is easy to understand why there is conflict between the two schools of thought.

Modern practice

Of course, there is no reason why the wet fly exponent cannot adopt the tactic of working upstream, and modern practice is very often to use just one fly on the leader— the point fly, in fact—and follow exactly the same tactics as the dry fly purist—working upstream and casting only to an observed fish. In such cases, the selected fly will almost always be a sound copy of a natural life form, preferably one which exists in good numbers in the particular fishery. Specific nymph copies can be excellent, as can shrimp patterns. In stillwater fishing, with no current to work the flies, the angler has to learn to

HOW TO MAKE YOUR OWN 'TEAM OF THREE' LEADER

Fly Line

Knotless Taper 48i

Needle Knot

0.020 in to 0.012 in approx.

Hill's Patent Cast Carrier, a neat and handy way of carrying made-up casts and teams of flies without tangling.

Eric Birch

manipulate the flies manually. When fishing from the bank, the choice of a floating line, or one or other of the sinking lines is the same as it is on the river. Whereas line selection on the river, however, may be dictated more by current speed than any other factor, on stillwaters the final selection may well be dictated by the depth of water in front of the angler, the depth at which the trout are feeding, and the speed of the retrieve required to induce a take.

What line to use?

If the trout are taking food close to the surface on slow moving food items, then a floating line and slow retrieve—or no retrieve at all—is indicated, and the take of an interested trout is signalled by a movement of the end of the line. Where the trout are deeper, and only willing to accept a fast moving object, it will be necessary to use a sinking line. Whether one uses a slow, medium or fast sinker is governed by the particular circumstances.

On the larger waters, lure fishing has come into prominence in recent years. Normal practice, almost invariably, is to attach one lure at the point of the leader and cast this out as far as possible by means of the double haul cast. Distances of 50 yards can be achieved with practice using this technique. A sinking line is usually employed, and retrieval tends to be very fast indeed, so fast that it is known as 'stripping'. Occasionally trout are willing to accept a lure stripped across the surface using a floating line, which

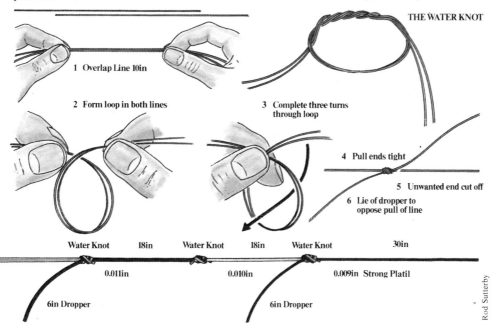

THE WATER KNOT

1 Overlap Line 10in

2 Form loop in both lines

3 Complete three turns through loop

4 Pull ends tight

5 Unwanted end cut off

6 Lie of dropper to oppose pull of line

Water Knot	18in	Water Knot	18in	Water Knot	30in
0.011in		0.010in		0.009in Strong Platil	
6in Dropper			6in Dropper		

Rod Sutterby

Wet fly fishing

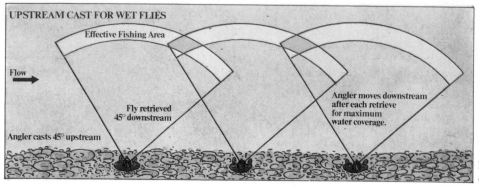

UPSTREAM CAST FOR WET FLIES

Effective Fishing Area

Flow

Angler casts 45° upstream

Fly retrieved 45° downstream

Angler moves downstream after each retrieve for maximum water coverage.

Rod Sutterby

P. H. Ward/Natural Science Photos

(Above) The upstream cast. (Left) A box of lures ideal for nymph fishing. (Below right) When the trout are not feeding on surface insects, the nymph can be fished sink-and-draw. Trout feeding on hatching flies might be tempted by one using the style shown in the lower illustration.

creates a pronounced wake behind the lure.

It seems to be less well known that a lure on a sinking line, fished so slowly that it bounces along the bottom, can be very productive, and often leads to the capture of larger trout. Where it is permitted, the static sunken fly can also prove very killing. This involves casting out a fairly heavily dressed lure on a medium sinking line, letting it sink to the bottom, and just waiting for a trout to snap it up. Sometimes the lure will be taken as it sinks, or is picked up off the bottom shortly after it has settled, but on other occasions one has to resort to an occasional short retrieve before allowing it to settle again. The bed of the lake has to be clear of weed and obstructions for this to be successful, and the water should preferably be at least 6ft deep.

Fishing the traditional 'team of three' from a boat can be very exciting. The method is to let the boat drift, casting before you, and retrieving line just fast enough that you keep in touch with your flies as the boat drifts towards them. Sometimes it pays to retrieve a little faster, so that the bob fly dibbles nicely along the tops of the waves. Sometimes a trout will take the bob fly so close to the boat that the angler can be completely taken by surprise.

Drift problems

Lures can be fished very efficiently from a boat, and so can a single fly or nymph, usually on a sinking line. If the boat drifts too quickly, this can create difficulties, so the normal practice is to slow down the rate of drift by using a drogue or 'sea anchor'—a cone of heavy canvas attached securely to a spreader ring, and allowed to trail over the side—acting as a brake. Alternatively, anchor the boat in a chosen position and fish in exactly the same way as one would fish from the bank.

Catching the biggest trout from reservoirs and very large lakes can be difficult because of the vast expanse of water that has to be covered. Fortunately, a great many small stillwater fisheries have opened up across the

118

country, and many of these have the twin attributes of possessing clear water and quite large trout. Usually it is more expensive to buy a day ticket on these small fisheries than it is on the reservoirs, but usually value for money is obtained because the average size of the fish is larger and the density of stock very much higher. The average angler catches one reservoir trout of about a pound in weight on each visit. On small fisheries the average is usually three trout weighing more than twice the reservoir average.

Many of the small fisheries have rules banning lure fishing, or the use of more than one fly on the leader. This makes sense because long casting on a small water is hardly ever necessary, and would interfere with the enjoyment of other anglers. Also, it is easier to persuade a good-sized trout to take an imitation of a natural insect than it is to get it to take a gaudy lure. The most successful anglers study the water very carefully, first of all to locate a trout, and secondly to try to see what it is likely to be eating. The more visits an angler makes to a particular water, the easier he finds it to locate his trout, and guess what the trout is feeding on—or likely to feed on. Once the trout has been seen, and the decision made

which fly to tie on, the angler casts his nymph or bug to that trout, just as the dry fly anglers does with surface-feeding trout.

This type of wet fly fishing is, however, a little more difficult than dry fly fishing because the trout might be feeding 6ft down from the surface and the angler has to be very accurate with his cast, not only to get the distance right, but also to know that his fly will sink fast enough to reach a trout before it moves on to feed elsewhere. If the water is very deep, it may be necessary to use a sink tip line, but usually it is sufficient to use a floating line with a long leader, and perhaps some lead wire added to the artificial fly when it is being dressed.

Salmon and the wet fly

Wet fly fishing for salmon can be grand sport, although usually very expensive. The usual practice is to make long casts across the river, let your fly drift downstream over likely holding areas, and then retrieve slowly. The flies are often very large—larger even than reservoir lures—and mostly look like nothing on earth. When the water is low, much smaller flies are used, with fairly sparse dressing, and indeed, it is probable that some of the more effective reservoir lures have been developed from low water salmon flies.

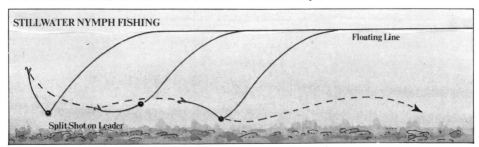

STILLWATER NYMPH FISHING

Floating Line

Split Shot on Leader

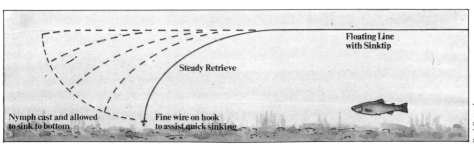

Floating Line with Sinktip

Steady Retrieve

Nymph cast and allowed to sink to bottom

Fine wire on hook to assist quick sinking

Rod Sutterby

Chalk stream fishing

During the middle of the 19th century the great traditions of dry fly fishing developed on the chalk streams of England, particularly on such world famous rivers as the Test, Itchen and Kennet, in the Southern Counties. Fortunately for the modern angler the purism associated with the use of the dry-fly-only rule to a large extent disappeared when nymph fishing was introduced in the early 1900s. Today, on many of our chalk streams, nymph fishing is only allowed after 1 July. This is a sensible rule, as hatches of surface fly during the height of summer are often minimal, and so the use of a nymph during this period at least provides the angler with some interesting and demanding fishing.

During the past 20 years fly fishing has developed enormously. Today, there are many thousands of anglers, proficient at casting a fly, who regularly fish on lakes and reservoirs. Many would undoubtedly love to fish a chalk stream but probably feel they are not sufficiently experienced. This is nonsense. If you can cast a fly delicately onto the water, the art of dry fly or nymph fishing on chalk streams can be quickly acquired.

Slow, stealthy approach

The angler must appreciate that he will be fishing in very clear water, which means the trout can see him from a considerable distance, so that the fly fisherman tramping along the bank looking for trout will scare more trout than he catches. A slow, stealthy approach to the water is essential and at times it may even be necessary to crawl and cast from a kneeling position to fish successfully from an open section of bank.

Of equal importance is the actual presentation of the dry fly or nymph. Use as

G. L. Carlisle.

RED-RIBBED OLIVE

RED SEDGE

LEADED SHRIMP

Lyn Cawley

(Above) Three typical flies for use in chalk stream fly fishing.
(Left) The Lambourne, a chalk stream tributary of the River Thames.

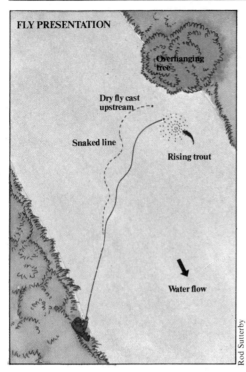

FLY PRESENTATION

Overhanging tree

Dry fly cast upstream

Snaked line

Rising trout

Water flow

Rod Sutterby

(Above) Trout, like many species of fish, are attracted by overhanging vegetation. So watch for rises and cover them by 'snake' casting beyond the rise. As the line straightens the fly will drift down to where the fish lies.

light a line as you can handle proficiently, plus a fine leader. Nothing will scare trout more than to have the fly line landing on the water within its field of view, or even the fly or nymph itself if it lands heavily.

When you have the choice of using either a dry fly or a nymph, it is best to decide beforehand which method you are going to employ on any given stretch of water. When fishing with a dry fly you should concentrate on looking for rise forms on the surface, but when using a nymph you should be looking into the water for feeding fish. It is not possible to combine the two successfully. Try to cast the fly so that it lands delicately, to one side of the fish or rise, or better still well upstream (although this will depend on your position relative to the trout).

A good general pattern

Many fly fishermen think that it is essential to have considerable knowledge of the natural flies that the trout may be rising to, so that a matching artificial may be used to deceive them. This is not strictly true; while it may be necessary for a particularly wary or difficult trout, a large proportion of fish will succumb to a good general pattern of dry fly. These include such names as 'Kites Imperial', 'Rough Olive', or 'Black Gnat' during the day, or as dusk approaches, a 'Lunns Particular' or a small 'Red Sedge'.

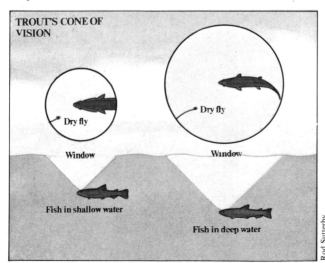

TROUT'S CONE OF VISION

Dry fly

Dry fly

Window

Window

Fish in shallow water

Fish in deep water

Rod Sutterby

(Left) Fish have a cone of vision which is related to the depth at which they are swimming. The smaller cone allows the trout less time to react to any unnatural movement of the fly or line. Here, the fly must drift across the trout's nose. With a deep-lying fish the fly should drift to one side of the trout. For objects above the surface, due to refraction, the deeper-lying fish will see the angler before the shallow-swimming trout does.

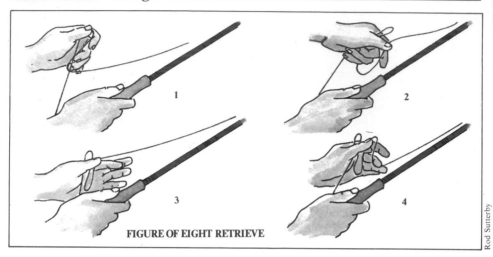

FIGURE OF EIGHT RETRIEVE

Rod Sutterby

During the latter half of the season, when hatches of surface fly are sparse and few trout are rising, it is necessary to use a nymph. This is because trout are feeding below the surface. In chalk streams the main underwater diet of trout is various species of olive nymph, although some trout may be observed searching the bottom or probing weed for shrimps. It is only necessary, therefore, to have an unweighted nymph to offer to fish feeding just below the surface, or a weighted 'Pheasant Tail' or 'PVC Nymph' to offer to deeper feeding trout. Where trout feed on shrimps in deep water a heavy-leaded shrimp pattern may be used. Weighted nymphs should be cast well upstream of a feeding trout and allowed to drift downstream.

Watch for the flash

It is often difficult to see the nymph underwater so it is important to watch for the flash of the fish as it turns to take the bait, or the wink of white as he opens his mouth, and strike immediately.

Should the trout consistently refuse your offering, try the 'induced take' technique. Correctly applied this technique can be a very efficient method, but it does require some expertise. When you think the nymph has appeared within the visual field of the trout, slowly raise the rod tip. This will make the nymph rise towards the surface—which most trout find irresistible.

(Above) The 'Figure of Eight' method of line recovery while fly fishing.
(Below) Fly fishing on chalk streams can be practised in the most attractive surroundings. Because of the nature of the gin-clear water the angler must always make a cautious approach.

S. L. Ward/Natural Science Photos

Reservoir fishing

Bill Howes

The reservoirs of Britain are all large expanses of water, averaging around 800-1,000 acres, with Grafham Water at 1,600 acres and the giant Rutland Water 3,200 acres.

With such large areas, the first problem is finding the fish. Not only might they be concentrated in a fairly small area, they could also be feeding at the surface, the bottom, or somewhere inbetween.

Weather conditions

When starting to fish any reservoir, the first consideration is the weather. If the wind has been blowing in a particular direction for several days previously, it is safe to assume that there will be fish around the windward bank. If the day is cloudy and overcast fish are more likely to be at the surface than if the

This angler took two fine rainbows from the 1,600-acre expanse of Grafham Water.

day is bright. Choose the method and place to fish accordingly.

When boat fishing, you can use a rudder or drift-controller if the reservoir rules allow. The method then would be to set the rudder so that the boat drifts along the bank, and to cast at right-angles to the boat. Allow the line to sink, and when it has gone through an arc and is straight behind the boat, retrieve your fly. Takes very often occur just as the fly is passing through the bend of the arc, because at this point it suddenly speeds up, and any fish following will often be fooled into taking it rather than let it escape.

If rudders are not allowed by the reservoir

Bill Howes

rules, one can control the rate of drift with a drogue—an attachment similar to a parachute in appearance—suspended in the water behind the boat to slow down the rate of drift. Similar tactics may be used with the drogue as with the rudder.

With both of these methods it is possible to cover a great deal of water, and if fish are not contacted within a reasonable space of time, it is advisable to change and fish a different depth. This is achieved by using either a slower or faster sinking line or allowing more or less time for the fly to sink.

Floating line tactics

If fish are seen to be rising or feeding just under the surface, it is obviously sound tactics to use a floating line and a team of nymphs or wet flies. These are fished very slowly, across the wind, with no movement whatsoever, except the movement given by the drift of the boat. Fish moving up wind are very susceptible to this method, and if none are caught quickly when you know you have covered them, change the fly, or grease or de-grease the leader in case you are not fishing at their depth.

If the boat is drifting fast, it is advisable to anchor in an area where fish are, and fish across the wind, again not retrieving.

Recommended flies are the Tiger Nymph, Buzzer Nymph, Black and Peacock Spider, Amber Nymph, Sedge Pupa, Greenwell's Glory, March Brown, Butcher, Dunkeld and Invicta. Of course there are others, but these flies usually score well anywhere and in most conditions.

If you do not often fish at anchor, it is a good idea to do so if the fish are obviously on the bottom or concentrated in a small area. On these occasions you will find that a small lure worked slowly through the water works well. Flies such as the Appetizer, Black Chenille, Church Fry, Baby Doll, Whisky Fly, Jack Frost, Matuka, and Sweeney Todd are very effective.

These methods work very well from a boat but can still be adopted if you are restricted to bank fishing. Make for the windward

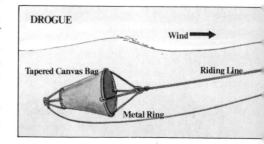

DROGUE

Wind

Tapered Canvas Bag

Riding Line

Metal Ring

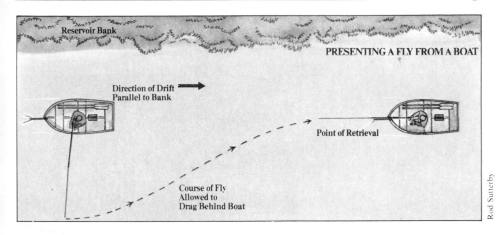

Reservoir Bank

Direction of Drift
Parallel to Bank

PRESENTING A FLY FROM A BOAT

Point of Retrieval

Course of Fly
Allowed to
Drag Behind Boat

Rod Sutterby

(Left) Early season trout fishing at a popular Midlands reservoir, Draycote. (Above) On the drift, a fly is cast at right angles, to finish up astern.

bank, and if there are bays there, so much the better. Standing on the point of a bay it is possible to cast across the wind with a team of nymphs or wet flies swinging round, as described previously.

If the water is deep from the bank, use a sinking line which will enable you to retrieve slowly without snagging, or a floating line with a long leader. That is, of course, if you need to fish deep. Use the same flies as you would when boat fishing.

Roving pays off

One spot from the bank might be fished very thoroughly, so if nothing is contacted, it often pays to move along. When the wind is blowing onto the bank, the wave action varies according to the depth of the water. In shallow water, more of the bottom is stirred up, which might attract feeding fish. This is

something always worth considering, so try all depths of water possible from the bank until you start catching.

As you will never know all about every reservoir you fish, consult local anglers when fishing a new water—it can save time.

Rutland Water

Of the many reservoirs in England, Rutland Water is certainly to be recommended. The fish there are fast-growing and hard-fighting, with a high average weight, and will come to all methods. After Rutland, Grafham must still rate highly in everyone's estimation because there is always the chance of a record-breaker, while Pitsford is very scenic and produces some beautiful brownies to nymph fishing tactics.

Chew is a large water with great potential, and neighbouring Blagdon is well established, and picturesque, with some very good fish. Both Chew and Blagdon can prove to be very difficult indeed, but are superb when going well.

Ravensthorpe is small but pretty, and some big fish have been caught there in the past, although good fish are rare now. Other reservoirs to recommend are Ardleigh and Hanningfield. These reservoirs tend to be favourites but it is also a good idea to visit others each season.

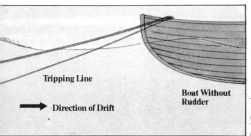

Tripping Line

Direction of Drift

Boat Without
Rudder

Rod Sutterby

Rudders are sometimes not allowed, so the drogue acts to stream behind the boat and slow the rate of drift.

125

Salmon fishing

For most experienced salmon anglers the epitome of skill in their sport comes, perhaps, in the months of May and June when the salmon are in a playful mood and will condescend to take very small flies fished on a floating line. This style of fishing is not as complex as it may appear and by far the most challenging aspect of the exercise is to be on the right river at the right time and place. This injects a degree of chance into the success or failure of salmon fishing and there are few short cuts to assist the novice.

Small flies, floating lines

Fly fishing with small flies and floating lines is one of the easiest and most successful forms of salmon fishing providing that the water temperatures have been sustained over the 10°C (50°F) mark for a few days; the water lacks an excess acidity and is clear and not excessively deep. The Aberdeenshire Dee is a classic example of a fly river, but there are many others where similar conditions are found.

Basically the fly is cast across the current and slightly downstream. The angler may

have to wade to successfully cover known lies, but the object is to make the fly pass over the lies slightly submerged as slow as possible to make it move. The take from a fish may appear as nothing more than a slow but solid draw. In any event it is a grave mistake to strike and it is quite normal for the salmon to merely hook itself as it pulls the fly. A hooked salmon has a few ideas of its own and the angler may expect to struggle with a fish for roughly one minute for each pound it weighs.

It cannot be stressed too strongly that the primary requirement is to know the salmon lies, what to do and when. Casting or placing the fly may be quickly learned, but it may take years to acquire knowledge of an area.

Spinning technique

Undoubtedly, the form of salmon fishing that requires the most practice is spinning with a double-handed rod and a fixed-spool or multiplying reel. This rechnique must account for the lion's share of all salmon

(Below) An angler enjoying autumn salmon fishing on the Tweed at Innerleithen.

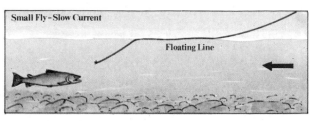

Small Fly – Slow Current

Floating Line

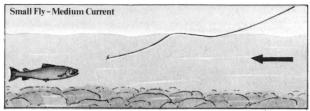

Small Fly – Medium Current

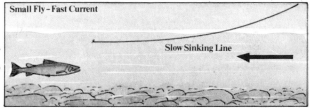

Small Fly – Fast Current

Slow Sinking Line

Arthur Oglesby

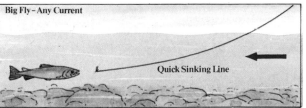

Big Fly – Any Current

Quick Sinking Line

Rod Sutterby

(Right) To be on the river at the right time is one of the essentials of salmon fishing. But then the fly, the line, the current, and the angler's skill must all combine to land the taking fish.

Selection of the lure for salmon fishing depends upon weight of the lure and the strength of the current.

Steve Bicknell

caught, but it is often over-used and abused and there are some rivers where its continued use may do more harm than good. It is a useful technique to apply in the early spring when the water is cold and deep and when the fish are reluctant to move far from their lies. At such times it is barely possible to make the bait move too slow and deep. Of course, it is not much fun to be continually hung up on the bottom, but if the right weight of bait has been chosen it should be possible to cast it across the current and have it swing round (just like our fly) without winding the reel handle. The current is generally strong enough to make the bait revolve. Any form of reel handle winding before the bait is out of the

127

current and dangling immediately downstream will make the bait move to fast and too high in the water.

Choosing the weight in the bait is therefore one of paramount consideration. The angler must assess current strength and depth and then choose a bait which, when cast across the current, will swing round at good depth without fouling the bottom and, in all but semi-stagnant water, without winding the handle of the reel. Good salmon baits are to be found in the wide range of Devon minnows, and the myriad of spoon baits on offer are available in a wide choice of colours. During the colder months there is rarely a call for baits smaller than 2in long.

Other methods

Although spinning and fly fishing form the basis of most salmon fishing technique there are several other legitimate methods which the angler may resort to when the going gets tough. It is possible to limit all

salmon fishing to small flies and floating lines in late spring and summer and big flies and sinking lines for early spring or late autumn. However, many times the worm, prawn or shrimp has saved an otherwise blank day or week. At certain times and seasons the use of these natural baits can be very effective, but there are still too many anglers who will resort to them without trying other more sporting methods.

It should not be implied that fishing with any of these natural baits is easy. There is a

This sequence illustrates the correct way of presenting a worm across salmon lies. Start upstream (1) to cover any possible fish. Move to 2, then down to position 3. If no salmon takes, move up to 4, then to 5, where a fish may be lying in front of the stone. Lastly try lie 6 on the far bank by casting out and letting line out to drift the worm down behind the obstruction.

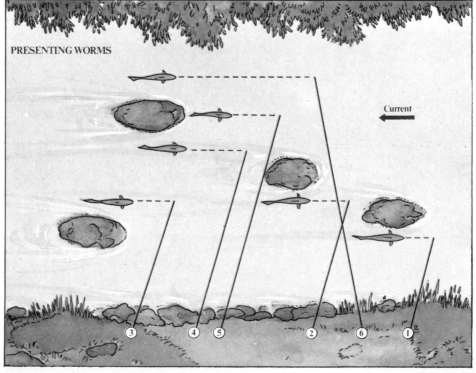

PRESENTING WORMS

Current

Rod Sutterby

sense in which successful fishing with a worm or prawn is more difficult than fly fishing, but there are times, conditions and situations when they might prove too effective and spoil the sport for others.

The same basic requirement for good weight assessment is necessary for successful worm fishing. The worm has to trundle over the bottom of the river and if the weight is too heavy there will be frequent hang-ups. If it is too light the worm may not get to the bottom.

Worm fishing

The best time for worm fishing is, perhaps, after a recent flood when the water is still coloured and higher than normal. The salmon may be laid quite close to the bank and there is again no substitute for knowing the waters. Whatever happens the angler must be at great pains not to strike at the first bite he detects. A salmon will frequently play with the worm for several minutes before taking or rejecting the bait.

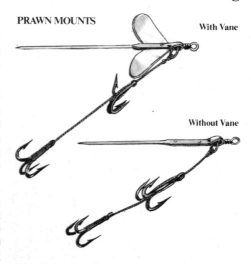

PRAWN MOUNTS

With Vane

Without Vane

(Above) Prawn mounts can be obtained with and without spinning vanes.
(Below) Shrimp and prawn can be used with spinning tackle and (bottom) with a float. Drift-lining without a float gives exciting and surprising fishing.

(Below) A spiral of lead wire above the swivel often helps to prevent snagging hooks on the bottom.

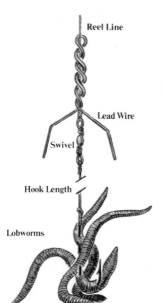

Reel Line

Lead Wire

Swivel

Hook Length

Lobworms

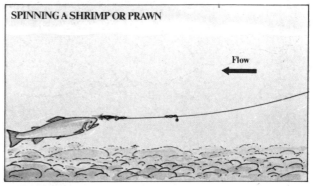

SPINNING A SHRIMP OR PRAWN

Flow

FLOAT FISHING WITH A SHRIMP OR PRAWN

Flow

Rod Sutterby

129

Sea trout fishing

A good motto for the angler seeking sea trout today would be, 'First find a sea trout river!' The sea trout's environment, like that of the salmon, is slowly being eroded; and where it abounds its runs and migrations tend to be more fickle and unpredictable than previously. So the angler must do some intensive homework: to find an adequate sea trout river and then, miraculously, contrive to be on the river when the ephemeral sea trout is in the pools of his own beat.

Many dedicated sea trout anglers feel that fly fishing for sea trout with a floating line presents the ultimate angling challenge in Britain today. This must be a matter of opinion and opportunity, but undoubtedly the sea trout is one of the shyest fish to inhabit our waters. For this reason, most sea trout fishing, in normal to low water, is done under cover of dusk or darkness.

The ideal sea-trout rod is single-handed and about 10ft long. It should be rigged with a No 7 double or forward taper line, attached to a 9ft monofilament leader of not less than

Fishing the tail of Polchrain, a pool on the River Spey noted for the excellence of its sea trout fishing.

Arthur Oglesby

6lb b.s. To this tie on a No 10 single or double-hooked fly. Add waders and net and the sea trout angler is ready for the fray.

Patterns of sea trout fly are as legion as the colours on Joseph's coat. Most anglers have their favourites, but there is little doubt that the angler is much more fussy in this respect than the fish. In the dark it sees the fly as only a vague silhouette, so it is size and not colour which is more important.

Wait for the signal

There is a magic about the eerie dusk of a summer evening. The best nights often come after a sharp but warm shower of rain, when it is cloudy rather than clear and a myriad of insects are dancing over the water. But do not be in a hurry to begin fishing, however; it is a mistake to start too early. While it is still light, and with a discreet reconnaissance, establish where the sea trout are lying—but do not assume that they will stay put as darkness descends. Initial activity from the fish often takes the form of splashing or surface rises. This is the signal to start. Concentrate at first on the streamier sections of the river and leave the quiet glides and tails until full darkness.

Make your first cast out to a point slightly downstream and across the current. Further casts will have to be made in the dark, so it pays to stick a small piece of cotton wool onto the line to indicate the correct amount

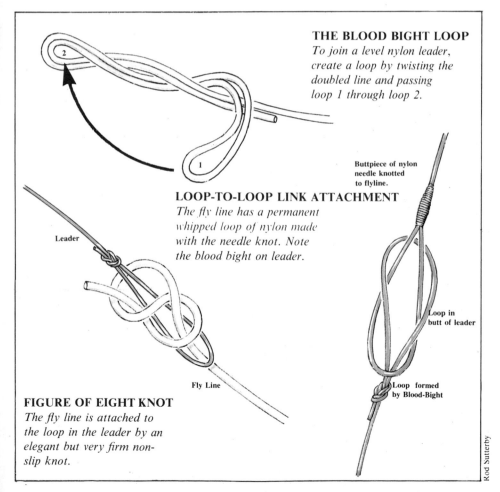

THE BLOOD BIGHT LOOP
To join a level nylon leader, create a loop by twisting the doubled line and passing loop 1 through loop 2.

Buttpiece of nylon needle knotted to flyline.

LOOP-TO-LOOP LINK ATTACHMENT
The fly line has a permanent whipped loop of nylon made with the needle knot. Note the blood bight on leader.

Leader

Loop in butt of leader

Loop formed by Blood-Bight

Fly Line

FIGURE OF EIGHT KNOT
The fly line is attached to the loop in the leader by an elegant but very firm non-slip knot.

Rod Sutterby

131

FALKUS' SUNK LURE

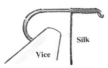

1. Put a few turns of silk (red) as seating on a short-shanked sneck bend hook.

2. Loop nylon round hook and pass both ends through eye. Nylon should be stiff enough to support hook without drooping.

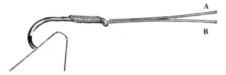

3. Whip nylon to hook shank and varnish.

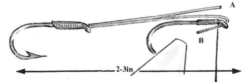

4. Wind a seating on a second hook, from about halfway on shank, forward to eye. Take Strand B through eye and whip silk back towards the point, tying in Strand B. Cut off B. Trim Strand A level with eye. Whip forward to eye, tying in Strand A along top of shank. Ensure hooks are in alignment.

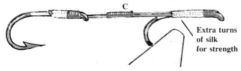

5. Whip nylon mount at C. Varnish mount. Paint hook shanks silver. Allow 2 days to dry.

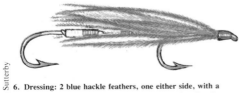

6. Dressing: 2 blue hackle feathers, one either side, with a few strands of peacock herl on top. Ensure that dressing extends only to point of tail hook. Apply red varnish to head.

Rod Sutterby

(Above) A 2lb sea trout caught from the Lune on a small fly and floating line.
(Left) The stages in tying Hugh Falkus's Sunk Lure, a night-fishing sea trout lure.

to use. With a little practice, the angler can sense when everything is going right, but even the experts experience the most diabolical tangles. When tangles happen, the best remedy is to retire well away from the water and, with the aid of a torch, exchange the leader and fly for another cast ready made up. Care must be taken not to let the torch beams show anywhere near the water. This can put sea trout down quickly.

Playing a spirited sea trout

On a good night, it is not long before the angler feels a determined tug. If the fish is properly hooked, there may then follow a hair-raising display when the fish seems to be more out of the water than in it. The rod suddenly arches into a taut bow, the fish pulling with frenzied runs and leaps. Fresh-run sea trout, however, have very tender

Arthur Oglesby

for the angler to take a brief rest, have a dram of whisky, and change his line for one that sinks. For the rest of the night a subsurface fly is generally the most productive lure.

Try a big tandem lure

After 0200hrs it is also worth while to try a big tandem lure fished deep. This lure represents a small fish and will often bring a response from some of the biggest fish in the water. The takes may be more gentle and delicate than to the subsurface fly, so all suggestions of an offer should be treated with a firm strike.

Not all sea trout fishing is practised at night. Following a good flood, when the water is falling and clearing, it is frequently possible to make good catches in daytime with the type of fly used for brown trout. This, however, is opportunist fishing in which it is essential to have quick access to good water and to be able to down-tools at a moment's notice and get to the river as soon as the keeper or gillie 'phones to say conditions are right. It is not usually long before the water is too clear for the shy daytime sea trout, but some good fish can be taken while murky conditions last.

Deadly baits

Other tactics involve spinners and worms. A small Mepps spoon is particularly good, spun in much the same way as for salmon. The $1\frac{1}{2}$in Devon minnow is a known killer in the Eden (Cumbria) and Border Esk. A worm is perhaps even more productive. Both can be deadly in slightly coloured water in daytime, but local knowledge of where to fish is essential, and this is not quickly learned by the casual visitor.

The fly, therefore, is not only the most aesthetically pleasing bait to most sportsmen, it is also the most effective sea trout method over a season. But the season is all too short. In many years it is possible to number on one hand those few nights when conditions are ideal. Such rarity prompted the anonymous comment that 'When conditions are right, there is nothing that will get the dedicated sea trout angler to bed—not even a new wife!'

mouths, and not all fish which pull at the fly are successfully hooked. Even many of those that are escape when the hook comes free during a twisting leap. The thrill of hooking and playing a spirited sea trout in the inky darkness never loses its excitement. The catch might be anything from $\frac{1}{2}$lb to a specimen topping 10lb, providing not only excellent sport but also gourmet fare.

Divide the night into three

The undisputed authority on sea trout fishing today is Hugh Falkus. In his book *Sea Trout Fishing* he divides the night into three distinct sections, which he calls 'first-half' (before midnight), 'half-time' (up to about 1 am), and 'second-half' (from 1 am until dawn). These periods reflect the changing habits of the sea trout during the night. The fish are active at the surface during the early night, retiring to deeper water after midnight. During the 'first-half', therefore, the angler should use a surface fly on a floating line. Then follows 'half-time' when the fish are uncooperative. This is the time

Fly fishing afloat

Most lake and reservoir trout fisheries provide boat fishing for those who prefer it. Many anglers would argue that the boat fisherman consistently catches more than his bank-fishing counterpart. Others heartily oppose this view. The majority choose according to prevailing conditions and what suits their pocket.

With half a gale blowing, the boat angler may find it impossible to fish either because the drift is too fast, or because the anchor will not hold bottom. It may then be wiser to stay on the bank, where some shelter may be found. Another day, he may find the bank lined with anglers, with hardly room to fish. If the water looks good he may decide to use a boat and take advantage of the greater freedom of movement this provides.

Some anglers travel light, prepared to walk the bank with only rod, reel and fly box—an excellent day's fishing if you are in the mood. Others carry a lot of gear to cover all the possible variations required. Then, a boat is very useful indeed.

Whatever your motives for fishing from a boat, there are a few essentials which will improve your chances. The most obvious is a good anchor. A length of regular or nylon rope about 30-50 yards long is indispensable, and a heavy lump of concrete attached by a ringbolt will suffice either to anchor, or to trail behind the boat in a high wind to slow the drift. A proper anchor is preferable, however, especially of the folding variety, which makes for easy stowage and portage when not in use.

Irish Tourist Board

The anchor rope should never be fastened to the rowlocks but must be taken twice around the thwart (the oarsman's bench) and fastened with a tucked half-blood knot. It can then be passed through a crutch or over the side direct, according to fancy. The anchor will always sit and hold better if it has about 6ft of light chain attached at the business end. This prevents the line being pulled upwards, and stops the anchor from dragging, except in a very high wind.

Usefulness of the drogue

A drogue is also very valuable for slowing down the rate of drift (see Small Boats feature). Anchor and drogue lines must be coiled neatly under their respective thwarts in readiness for use, and the drogue should be fitted with a trip-rope to help pull it in when no longer needed.

If you have ever lifted an oar to get it inboard and found that the crutch is inadvertently caught on the oar, lifted from its socket, and neatly dropped over the side into 20ft of water, you will not need to be reminded that a couple of split pins made of fence-wire slipped through the holes provided, can be valuable to secure crutches in their sockets. These are easy to remove at the end of the day, but be sure to stow them in your bag when setting off.

Finally, you should carry a lifejacket or support of some kind, against emergencies.

On many waters it is mandatory to carry the boat cushions provided, and these are designed to double as life-savers. Many anglers feel it worthwhile to have their own, for they provide the comfort needed on a hard thwart, and in emergencies they may save a life.

The cost of a boat normally demands that you should share it with a friend. Such friends must be chosen for their tact, and their capacity to sit silently in a boat, for nothing is worse than having to share a boat with a noisy idiot.

Occasionally, you meet a partner who is left-handed and provided you are right-handed the two of you can have the best of both worlds, neither having to cast across the boat. Otherwise, you should change seats at intervals so that you both get a share of the best position. Unless you are both experienced at changing seats while afloat, take the boat ashore to do so.

Do not stand up

It is surprisingly common to see anglers fishing from a standing position in a boat. This can be dangerous (and ill-mannered if you are sharing the boat). Those who are most accustomed to boats rarely, if ever, do it. Unless the boat is large (unlike those on most reservoirs), avoid standing up.

Depending on conditions, there is a choice for basic methods of fly fishing from a boat.

(Left) The enjoyment of fly fishing from a boat. Here, on White Lake, Co Westmeath, Ireland, the angler is properly seated, his boat not cluttered with too many items of unnecessary equipment. With the soft breeze on his back and the fish rising, the day is perfect.
(Right) Short-lining, when fishing the drift, gives one the chance to use the dropper well, skittering it on the surface.

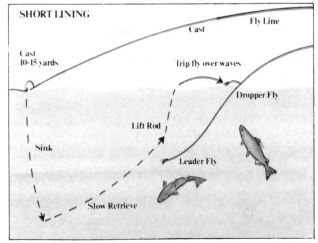

SHORT LINING

Cast

Fly Line

Cast 10-15 yards

Trip fly over waves

Dropper Fly

Lift Rod

Sink

Leader Fly

Slow Retrieve

Rod Sutterby

Fly fishing afloat

(Left) A quiet corner on a Midlands reservoir. While the angler fishes the drift, parallel wind lanes could be the clue to feeding fish.
(Right) How two anglers can cover the maximum area in front of a drifting boat.
(Below right) A happy angler with five stock trout from Sundridge Lake, one of the many prolific Kent waters.

Bill Howes

The commonest and best-known is simply to fish the drift. This is most suitable when the wind is not too strong, and when fish are known, or believed, to be feeding on or near the surface. When fish are sought on or near the bottom it is better to fish at anchor, which enables you to pause for the fly to sink properly before retrieving it. In strong wind conditions, dapping is a useful alternative, and when the water is still, with a mirror-like surface, it may be expedient to use the dry fly.

Assess the wind direction first

When fishing the drift, it is usual to assess the wind direction and row to a starting position estimated to allow the boat to drift in a course which avoids bank anglers, but at the same time covers the major headlands, or waters where known weedbeds or alternate shallows and deeps hold fish. If a long, uninterrupted drift can be established, it is often very effective, but it is frequently necessary to take short drifts, rowing upwind to resume a parallel of similar drift.

When the wind is fairly brisk boat anglers usually look about for wind lanes caused by headlands, woods, or shoreline contours which affect the wind. Wind lanes can generally be seen quite clearly as areas where the wind creates long strips less broken than the surrounding water. This effect is usually due to relatively less wind turbulence on the surface, and since it often causes large numbers of wind-borne creatures to be deposited there, fish soon learn to feed along

these areas, and can indeed often be seen moving among them. To fish such a lane on the drift entails placing the boat at the head of the lane, drifting with the drogue out, and occasionally giving the oars a tweak in one direction or the other to keep in the lane.

Sooner or later, the drifting boat arrives on the shore at the end of the drift and it is necessary to row upwind again to resume. In high winds this can be a daunting business, requiring a sustained and lengthy pull at the oars. There is usually one bank at least slightly sheltered from the wind, and the tactic is to set the boat across wind at an angle, rowing gently enough to hold your position and allowing the the wind to 'sail' you into the sheltered bank. Once in the lee of the bank, you can usually row up with little effort, taking advantage of bays and inlets and only venturing into the wind when you have to pass headlands. When the boat is sufficiently upwind, you can take up position for the next drift.

Fishing the drift usually entails what is called 'short lining', which means making casts of 10-15 yards only, then giving the fly time to submerge before retrieving it slowly. As the fly reaches a midway position, the rod is raised slowly, bringing the dropper fly up to break surface. This is then tripped across the surface by further raising the rod and retrieving line as required. The fly is thus made to trip from wave to wave in a very effective manner. Often fish will slash at the

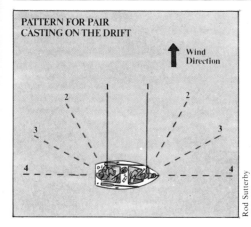

PATTERN FOR PAIR CASTING ON THE DRIFT

Wind Direction

Rod Sutterby

dropper, and then the rod top must be lowered slightly to allow the fish to turn before striking. Fishing the surface in this manner can be very successful, and if two anglers each fish a team of three flies, at least to begin with, it often enables them to establish the taking fly or flies.

The rate of retrieve can, of course, be varied at intervals, and an occasional longer cast serves to clear any twists imparted to the line by short lining. Anglers must cast alternately to avoid tangles during the back cast, and each should keep his fly in his own sector and avoid poaching. Casts should be fanned out to cover the whole of the sector to ensure that the water over which you drift is thoroughly explored.

Dapping rests the arm

Short lining demands almost continuous casting and can eventually be very tiring. For a change it is useful to change over to dapping for a spell. This is best carried out with a long dapping rod fitted with a nylon or floss silk dapping line, but it can be done with light fly lines if the wind is brisk. The technique is to get the fly hovering a few inches above the surface, at intervals dropping it on the top to float or simply touch. Fish can often be seen following the fly before it alights, and they frequently take with a thump the moment it touches down. It requires considerable control not to strike such a fish too soon and the golden rule is to *see* it turn first.

If the wind dies off altogether, fish will often refuse the fly that accurately covers them, especially when it is towed across them with a great wake which, in the clear undisturbed water, makes the cast look like a wire hawser. In these conditions it is often profitable to switch to the dry fly, fishing a line greased to within an inch of the fly, which is positioned and left to simulate the natural insect. Takes are often sudden and powerful, and if your rod is inadvertently pointed towards the fly, you risk being smashed on the take.

When the boat fisherman really needs to fish the bottom, he must almost invariably anchor. Then fishing a sinker and making fairly lengthy casts may pay off, a method similar to that adopted by bank anglers fishing the bottom. Perhaps the greatest danger for the boat angler is his tendency to create powerful rocking movements of the boat which send out shock waves and put down fish. If you cannot make lengthy casts without this, you would do better to fish a medium or shortish line.

Bill Howes

The evening rise

The evening rise is that special time towards evening, usually just before or after dusk when, attracted by failing light and a profusion of food, the trout begin to feed in earnest on or near the surface. Their behaviour is advertised by their continual rising, sloshing, topping and tailing, or cruising with backs awash. The evening rise conjures a picture of solid thumps, dancing rod tips, screeching reels, and anglers scooping up fish in all directions.

Yet, the sober fact is that the evening rise is an angler's fondly cherished myth—a delusion originating in the days when a few lucky anglers fished the famous chalk streams in a semi-pastoral England that no longer exists.

Most trout anglers today fish large lakes and reservoirs stocked with farm-bred, pellet-fed trout which prefer, ignoring the rules, to feed on the bottom, rather than on the surface in traditional style. They often fail to rise in the evening or at any other time. So on lakes and reservoirs you cannot depend on such a rise, even when wind, temperature, humidity and millions of floating insects seem to demand it.

Magic of the evening rise

Perhaps this accounts for the sheer magic of an evening rise when it *does* happen. There are few more awesome sights and sounds for the angler than the plop, sip, or splosh of rising fish all about him, especially when the sun is just disappearing behind distant trees, the atmosphere is tinted with red, and great widening ripples spread across a blood-coloured surface.

It is idyllic and might last ten minutes or an hour, but the magic may be tinted with sheer frustration and fury. To many anglers

Irish Tourist Board

it also means a chance of a face-saver after a daunting day with no sign of a fish moving, and with nothing but a weary arm and an aching back that is miraculously cured for the duration of the rise. Despite the evening rise, many will still finish the day empty handed, while others will take the limit.

The anticipation

Up to a point, you can sometimes anticipate the evening rise. When you see and hear buzzers hatching and flying freely during the afternoon, you can often expect at least a localised buzzer rise coinciding with dusk, or shortly after it. Now is the time to fish a buzzer team of red, white and blue nymphs (or any other colour for that matter) for you may with patience, skill, and a bit of luck coax a couple of fish to the net. Alternatively, when sedge flies appear in great clouds and start out towards the ripple line, you can expect the trout to start slaughtering them at any moment. You must then try longhorns, silverhorns, black sedges, red sedges or greys, although sometimes you do better with the larvae or their imitations. Whether to fish wet or dry adds to the dilemma.

If your clothing is covered with tiny white-winged flies which also carpet the water, you can expect a maddening rise of fish to take the *Caenis*—the well-named 'Angler's curse'.

(Above) Before the evening rise there is a period of calm, quiet anticipation.
(Left) A still evening on Lough Corrib.
(Below) This evening the rise was not a myth. It occurred, and a trout is netted.

The evening rise

Often on such occasions the trout splash and leap at the insects on the water but you need more than skill and luck to take fish then whatever you try to catch them on.

Sometimes it is just possible, if your eyesight is excellent and your entomology better, to discern which fly the fish are actually taking. But whether they will accept your imitation is quite another matter. By the time you've tried all the possibilities in terms of fly and tactics, you may have pricked several fish without netting one, although, alternatively, your skill and finesse may have brought you several to the net. Soon the rise is over either way, or perhaps the fish decide to eat something else which you failed to recognize earlier.

At other times, it is quite impossible to tell which is the taking insect on the water. At the same time it is usually too dark to see what comes out on the marrow spoon, so you cannot find out what the fish are eating that way either.

Don't panic!

Unfortunately, as your vision deteriorates in the half light, the fish see better. The problem of changing a fly in these conditions calls for nimble fingers, great care and good sight. It is easy to get into a panic deciding whether to fish wet or dry, and once flustered you are likely to ruin your cast to the only rise within reach. It takes nerve not to strike too soon when a take does occur—and more than a touch of luck not to hook the only bush within 50 yards on your back cast!

Before the light disappears completely you should examine your rig, especially if you are bold enough to fish more than one fly. It would not be unusual to discover that you have been fishing a ball of nylon with your artificial flies apparently mating in the middle of it.

Despite the disappointments, however, there are evening rises which make it all worth while. On these too rare occasions the fish bite unfussily and profusely. A fish may be hooked by an angler on your right, followed by another on your left. You enquire to discover that one took a Bloody

Irish Tourist Board

(Above) As the evening rise begins, the fly box is searched for the artificial.
(Right) Eric Horsfall Turner fishing the Lune on a spring evening.
(Below) Scott's Fancy, not an artificial Caenis but another 'Angler's Curse'.

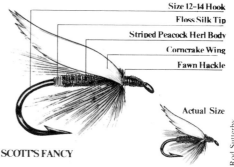

Size 12–14 Hook
Floss Silk Tip
Striped Peacock Herl Body
Corncrake Wing
Fawn Hackle

Actual Size

SCOTT'S FANCY

Rod Sutterby

Butcher and the other a Coachman. Should you change to one of these? As you hesitate, you get a great thump on your Mallard and Claret and you land the trout and fish on as before. Should you fish dry? Would a nymph be better? You catch another fish and suddenly the rise is over.

Over or not, all along the bank dozens of anglers are patiently fishing the water with every fibre of their being. Anglers are optimistic people, and rarely stop before it is simply too dark to fish on. But the memory of the evening rise persists all the way home.

Arthur Oglesby

Trout autopsies

A most important aspect of trout fishing which many anglers are inclined to overlook is the performing of autopsies on trout. To the uninitiated this may seem an unnecessary chore, and many fly fishermen tend to think that the examination of the stomach contents of a trout is a particularly scientific operation best left to the trained angler-entomologist. In fact, nothing could be further from the truth, for with the right tool and a basic knowledge of the more common insects, this is a comparatively simple task.

History of autopsies

The history of autopsies in trout fishing can be traced back several centuries. The method, then, was to slit open the belly of the dead trout exposing the stomach contents. As this was rather a messy business, it was eventually realized, as trout fishing progressed, that a slim spoon could be utilized. The spoon was inserted into the mouth of the fish and pushed into the stomach cavity, thereby removing its contents for examination. The present-day method is basically the same, except that the simple spoon has evolved over the years into an effieient piece of equipment generally referred to as the Marrow Scoop.

Various designs of scoop

Various shapes and designs are now obtainable, including a recent innovation made of clear plastic and fitted with a rubber bulb to suck the contents out of the stomach. Whichever tool is used, a small shallow glass dish is needed in which to transfer the contents. This should be filled with water as it helps separate the partly digested contents and makes identification easier. The object of the operation is to discover on what particular species of insect the trout may be feeding so that an appropriate pattern of artificial fly may be mounted.

It may take a little time for the average angler to become reasonably proficient at recognizing the many species of insects on

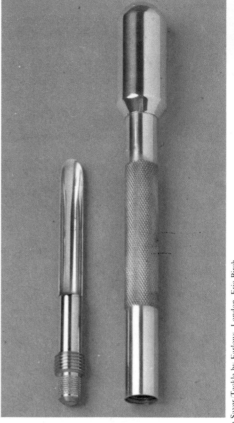

Kim Sayer/Tackle by Farlows, London. Eric Birch

which trout feed, but many books are available on the subject. To start with, it is a good plan to familiarize oneself with some of the more common fauna such as shrimps, louse, snails, midge larvae, daphnia, demersal nymphs or olive nymphs—and so on. Precise identification of the various species of upwinged flies, sedge flies, sedge pupae or midge pupae can follow at a later stage when the angler becomes more proficient.

Autopsies are not always positive. In some cases the stomach cavity may be empty because trout often regurgitate while they are being played; or perhaps they may not have fed for a long period. But the stomach is usually packed with food, and the angler can quickly establish their diet during the last 24 hours. To ascertain on which species the fish has been feeding immediately prior to capture, the angler must look for the specimen that appears the more intact.

While autopsies may be performed on fish other than trout, it is generally accepted to be of more value to the trout fisherman. It also follows that it is more important to fly fishers on stillwaters than to those on rivers. The

(Left) Objects needed for an autopsy: priest to dispatch the trout and marrow scoop to extract stomach contents. (Below-left to right) Results: a stomach pump used on a brown trout, and no need for a spoon as shrimps are found in the mouth.

majority of rivers capable of supporting a good head of trout are relatively clear, and it is usually possible to see on what they are feeding. On other occasions when trout are taking surface fly, specimens can be quickly captured to establish identity. On fast rocky rivers in hilly country, where the wet fly is used extensively, and it is difficult to see below the surface, autopsies can be of considerable assistance.

Selective food habits

On reservoirs and large lakes it is physically impossible, except on rare occasions, to see on what the trout are feeding, so when the angler arrives at the waterside he often has a problem in deciding which pattern of artificial fly to use. He can make a sensible guess, according to the time of the year, or if the water is familiar to him, can known from past seasons' experience roughly what to expect. Even so, there can be no certainty that the angler has made the correct choice. Trout tend to be selective and during any month there will be a wide variety of species from which they can choose. The only certain way to know which species the trout is choosing is to perform an autopsy.

First you have to catch your trout. A good plan, particularly if you are unfamiliar with the water, is to use a general attractor pattern such as a Mallard and Claret, Dunkeld or Invicta, to mention but three of the many popular general artificials available.

Robin Fletcher

John Goddard

Arthur Ogelsley